To Robert
with love
from
Jennifer
Sept 2011

The Day-mare.

Map of Ireland for *Lewis's Atlas of Ireland*, 1837

An Admiral's Eye View

SKETCHES OF IRELAND
BY LORD MARK KERR

Sycamore tree Glenarm Castle   25 SEPTEMBER 1838

ULSTER HISTORICAL FOUNDATION
2010

My thanks go foremostly to Hector McDonnell for lending me albums containing Mark Kerr's Irish drawings, and for permission to reproduce these images and other Kerr material in his possession. He also gave me a copy of his unpublished biography of this fascinating man, wrote the introduction to this volume, and provided text to accompany many of the drawings. I am also deeply indebted to Tom McNeill, Fred Hamond, Ian Montgomery, Annesley Malley, Malachy McSparran and Alex Blair for entering so well into the spirit of the project and composing such illuminating contributions. It was a privilege to share in their deep knowledge of their respective subjects. Frederick O'Dwyer kindly gave me the benefit of his extensive researches into the work of Christopher Myers, and Danny McGill shared the results of his ongoing work into the history of Ballycastle. Terence Reeves-Smyth of the Northern Ireland Environment Agency DOENI generously provided me with scanned images of the majority of the Kerr drawings, whilst Philip Doughty supplied a copy of his unpublished revision of Peter Rhodes's *The Antrim Coast Road*. My thanks also to the Public Record Office of Northern Ireland and Viscount Dunluce for permission to reproduce Kerr drawings or family portraits in their possession. Wendy Dunbar brought expertise, flair and infinite patience to the design work, and together we strove to ensure that the drawings appeared to best advantage.

The book could not have come into being without the support of the Ulster Historical Foundation and the generous sponsorship of the Esmé Mitchell Foundation, the Belfast Natural History and Philosophical Society and the Enkalon Foundation.

For Dick Oram,
to whom I owe so much

Ulster Historical Foundation is pleased to acknowledge support for this publication provided by the Belfast Natural History and Philosophical Society, the Esmé Mitchell Trust and the Enkalon Foundation. All contributions are gratefully acknowledged.

First published 2010
Ulster Historical Foundation
49 Malone Road, Belfast BT9 6RY

Except as otherwise permitted under the Copyright, Designs and Patents Act 1988, this publication may only be reproduced, stored or transmitted in any form or by any means with the prior permission in writing of the publisher or, in the case of reprographic reproduction, in accordance with the terms of a licence issued by The Copyright Licensing Agency. Enquiries concerning reproduction outside those terms should be sent to the publisher.

© Anne Casement, 2010
ISBN 978-1-903688-81-6

Printed by W & G Baird
Design by Dunbar Design

CONTENTS

The Irish Drawings of Lord Mark Kerr vii
A Tour of Ireland through the eyes of Lord Mark Kerr 1
Select Bibliography 103
Index 106

Vice Admiral,
The Lord Mark Robert Kerr. R.N.

by

Miss Sneyd.

in 1825

at Keel Hall,

in

Staffordshire.

The Irish Drawings of Lord Mark Kerr

HECTOR McDONNELL

Glenarm Park
from my window
13 OCTOBER 1835

Lord Mark Kerr, the creator of these drawings, was born in 1776, the third son of the 5th Marquess of Lothian, a wealthy Scottish peer. From an early age he showed an aptitude for drawing and painting, and as an adult became a remarkably interesting artist, producing a large number of fantastical drawings, as well as numerous topographical works. It was a somewhat unexpected gift, as there were no artistic leanings in his family background. His immediate ancestors had had fairly unexceptional military careers, and a long, if equally unexceptional, association with the Stuart Court. Admittedly his mother's family showed more flair. Her father's first cousin created an extraordinary park at Dangan in County Meath, crammed with follies, temples and two dozen obelisks, not to mention several exotic boats and a twenty-ton model warship on a lake, which was also equipped with island forts. His grandson was Arthur Wellesley, the general who broke the Napoleonic war machine and became the Duke of Wellington.

At sixteen, Mark Kerr entered the Royal Navy, in which he served from 1792 to 1805. He commenced his career as a midshipman on HMS *Lion*, the vessel which carried Lord Macartney as George III's ambassador to the court of Peking. There were scientists, linguists, musicians, astronomers, and botanists in the embassy's retinue, and several artists and draughtsmen. The finest artist, William Alexander, must have been an important influence on Mark Kerr, and under the tutelage of Henry Parish, the expedition's geometer, he learnt the essential skills of surveying and accurate depiction of coastal land profiles, which added considerably to his artistic abilities. By the time the *Lion* returned in 1794, war had been declared against revolutionary France. In the course of this conflict Kerr rose to captain the frigates *Cormorant* and *Fisgard*, and subsequently reached the rank of vice-admiral. Whilst in command of these ships his artistic life blossomed, and he produced several jewel-like, minute watercolours and drawings of naval life, including ones of his cabin, the beautifully ordered ropes on the orlop deck, the various codes for signalling with flags, and views of many of the places they visited, including Jersey, Toulouse, Gibraltar, Minorca and Portugal.

Lord Mark Kerr (1776–1840) painted by Margaret Carpenter, c. 1810.

COURTESY OF VISCOUNT DUNLUCE

When a temporary peace was made with Napoleon in 1799, Mark Kerr married the nineteen-year-old Lady Charlotte McDonnell, the younger of two Irish sisters, joint-heiresses to the estates of their father, the 6th Earl of Antrim, who had no legitimate male heirs. A few months earlier Charlotte's sister, Anne Catherine, who was Countess of Antrim in her own right, had married the wealthy, albeit dissolute, Sir Harry Vane-Tempest of Wynyard Park, County Durham. George III had permitted the Antrim family title and estates to pass through the female line for the sisters' generation, but they were then to pass solely to their male heirs. To her intense frustration, Anne Catherine had only one child, a daughter, whereas the Kerrs soon had several sons. As a result there were considerable family tensions, resulting in acrimonious law suits, and for a time the sisters could not even speak to each other.

The Antrim McDonnell family is descended from those great Scottish Clandonald chieftains of the Middle Ages, known as the Lords of the Isles. The younger brother of one lord married the heiress of an Anglo-Norman family, the Bissets, circa 1400, and thanks to this alliance, and some skulduggery, their descendants gained control of the Bisset lands, the Glens of Antrim. Through further adroit uses of both marriage and the sword they then extended their rule over the area between Larne and Coleraine, and the ruins of their many strongholds still line the coast. Fortunately for these McDonnells (as the Clandonald family name came to be spelt in Ireland) all these lands were granted by James 1 to Randal McDonnell, the head of this Irish Clandonald family. Randal subsequently bought himself the title of earl of Antrim, and in spite of all the upheavals of the following century, and many outbursts of extravagance, a large part of the original grant survived, and was still in the family's possession in Mark Kerr's time.

Lady Charlotte's half of the Antrim estates comprised chiefly the town of Ballymoney and much of the surrounding land, the town of Portrush and coastal townlands as far east as Bushmills, and significant portions of the parishes of Ardclinis and Layd. These

Charlotte, Lady Mark Kerr (1779–1835) painted by an unknown artist, c. 1805.
COURTESY OF VISCOUNT DUNLUCE

Anne Catherine, Countess of Antrim (1775–1834) painted by Hugh Douglas Hamilton, c. 1800.
COURTESY OF VISCOUNT DUNLUCE

Larne

View of Cave Hill. from the dining-room window. Belvoir. Ireland

Belvoir. Ireland

Fairhead Benmore from my Bedroom Window Clare Park
6 SEPTEMBER 1838

Ballycastle

lands, in the days before the Married Women's Property Acts, were technically-speaking Mark Kerr's, and documents of the time refer to him as the owner, not his wife. Nonetheless it is clear that Charlotte took a leading part in the administration of her estates, and that Kerr saw his role as merely an administrator and trustee, and would never have acted contrary to her wishes. The Kerrs did not have a house of their own within Charlotte's estates, and instead made their home in England, firstly in rented accommodation, and later at Holmwood, a sizeable house near Henley-on-Thames. They only came to Ireland for occasional extended visits, and usually stayed with friends or relations. The first of these visits took place only a few months after their marriage, when they were invited by a family connection, Lady Louisa Connolly, to spend the Christmas season at Castletown in County Kildare. She was of an older generation, but became a great friend, and stayed with them several times in England.

Mark Kerr did a few slight drawings during their time at Castletown, and his enthusiasm for the Irish landscape only really commenced during their next visits in 1802 and 1805, when they stayed at Belvoir Park, County Down, which belonged to Charlotte's half-brother, the 5th Viscount Dungannon. The fruit of these stays was a series of fine watercolours and drawings of the house and its environs. By the time of their next visit, in 1809, Belvoir had been sold, and they stayed instead at Clare Park near Ballycastle, the home of Charles McGildowney, the elder brother of Charlotte's agent, Edmund. Mark Kerr obviously became very much a part of Ballycastle society, and made many friendships in the maritime community clustered around the harbour. In his correspondence with John Casement of Ballycastle, another agent retained by the Antrim family, he asked engagingly to be remembered to 'all my old friends at the Quay'. John Casement was married to Charles and Edmund McGildowney's sister, and his uncle owned lands a short distance inland from Ballycastle.

ix

View in the County of Antrim of the Ruins of the ancient castle at Ballycastle, Fairhead and the Island of Rathlin in the distance

For a time the Kerrs had an established pattern for their Irish visits – for a month or so they would be at Clare Park, and then they would spend several more months staying with various friends and relations with large houses. It was typical of their time and class to make many expeditions of this sort during the year, and it would also have been normal to bring with them not only some of their children, but also the necessary servants to look after them. Often there would have been quite a large party of people staying in these houses, and the guests would be kept entertained by excursions, visits to neighbours, and all the normal country pursuits. As well as this they would have been expected to produce entertainments for everybody's amusement, from charades to plays, concerts and outdoor games. From the records I have been able to assemble, it seems that the Kerrs frequently spent almost half of every year making visits of this sort, and wherever they went Mark Kerr would produce drawings of what they saw, partly for himself, but presumably also for the amusement of his fellow guests. He seems to have frequently brought albums of his drawings and watercolours with him to these house-parties, and so could have produced them for examination on demand.

The Kerrs made three long stays in Ballycastle when their elder children were growing up. Doubtless there was plenty of estate business to be done with their agent, but it is easy to understand how much their young family would have relished the opportunity to be beside the sea, and visit places associated with their mother's family, especially when such excursions involved exciting boat trips, or stomach-turning views of fishermen crossing the flimsy bridge at Carrick-a-Rede. During these stays, Mark Kerr sketched many of the local scenes, and made forays by boat to other outstanding nearby landmarks, such as the Giant's Causeway, Dunluce Castle and Rathlin Island. He must have been attracted to these subjects because of their links with his wife's family, but, being a child of the late eighteenth century, he was also drawn by their romantic and picturesque qualities, and association with characters and events of long-ago, both mythical and real. His many drawings of monstrous creatures, and passion for creating fanciful garden follies

We 3 Monsters B.
My Father the Bishop
My Uncle the Judge
and me

Disappointment
He staid too long abroad – she adorned herself to bring him back – was fortunate enough to meet him on his return. Alas with – Two Sons!!

and sculpture, are testimony to his penchant for an 'other world' peopled by imaginary, grotesque, beings.

At some stage Mark Kerr also produced an elaborately worked-up watercolour of Ballycastle, nestling amongst its dramatic surroundings, but as it is undated we cannot be certain when it was produced. He clearly loved the town and surrounding area, and put more effort into this watercolour than he did for those of anywhere else in the British Isles, apart from the ones of Belvoir Park. Indeed the only other topographical watercolours which are so arduously worked up are the ones he produced on his voyage to China. I suspect, therefore, that the Ballycastle watercolour probably dates from fairly early on in his artistic life.

By contrast Mark Kerr's pen and wash or pencil sketches vary greatly in quality and accuracy. Some are carefully worked, accurate representations of their subjects, whilst others are little more than vague impressions. The majority of them were presumably done in situ when time was limited and family and other commitments made frequent demands on Kerr's attention. In some instances, such as the 1811 studies of Dunseverick, he seems to have injected an element of fantasy into his images, whilst the accuracy of others, in particular many of the later ones, may have been impaired either by having been completed afterwards from memory, or by difficulties resulting from deteriorating health or vision. Perspective and scale may also have been sacrificed on occasion to the need to create an attractive composition or picturesque image.

One of the striking features of Kerr's drawings of ancient Irish monuments is how closely they resemble their appearance today. Most of the ruined castles and churches we are familiar with are known to have been in use in the early seventeenth century, and their destruction most likely happened during the turmoil of the succeeding fifty years. Once they had been abandoned, any valuable or reusable materials would have been systematically removed or quarried out for use elsewhere. This resulted in the loss of virtually all the roofs, timbers and cut-stone surrounds to the doors and windows, leaving only the less desirable rubble and mortar cores of the main walls standing. These were generally solidly built, and those that did not collapse or get pulled down around the time of the buildings' abandonment have mostly decayed only gradually, with the result that many of the ruins still look remarkably as they did in Mark Kerr's time.

During their married life, the Kerrs made eight trips to Ulster, nearly always visiting Ballycastle, and the Massereene family at Antrim Castle and Londonderrys at Mount

Dunseverick, 18 August 1811

xi

Stewart, to both of whom they were connected by marriage. Mercifully, relations between Charlotte and her elder sister improved after the termination of their legal battles in 1814. Sir Harry Vane-Tempest, who had detested the Kerrs for their attempts to establish their rights to his wife's property, died in 1813, and four years later Anne Catherine married the impecunious and low-born Edmund Phelps. Charlotte was horrified by her sister's choice, seeing Phelps only as a despicable adventurer, particularly after he changed his surname to McDonnell. Despite this, Mark Kerr and Edmund McDonnell became close, doing their best to reconcile the sisters, and settle any remaining difficulties over the inheritance amicably. After their marriage, Edmund insisted his wife sell her London house and move to Glenarm, where they could live more quietly and economically. He obviously was delighted with his new home, and took the lead in improving the castle, its grounds and the neighbouring village of Glenarm.

Glenarm Castle from the Park

A Gentleman of High Family.

This Portrait is drawn on a Scale of an Inch to a foot – and tho' – the person was not considered tall in his own family yet he measured 12 Feet 4 Inches without his Shoes.

The seal on the reconciliation was set in 1828 when the Kerrs stayed with Anne Catherine and Edmund at Glenarm for the first time. Such was the success of this experiment that the Kerrs spent long periods at Glenarm on subsequent visits to the province. Anne Catherine died in 1834 and Charlotte a year later. Their widowers remained on very friendly terms, and Mark Kerr's last visit to Ulster was in 1839. He died in 1840. After his death, Letitia Louisa, his unmarried eldest daughter, compiled and captioned three volumes of his topographical drawings, entitling them *Scratches from Nature,* stuck his fantastical drawings into a series of fresh albums, carefully indexed, and left all of his artistic works to a niece, who subsequently passed them on to her descendants. This ensured their preservation, but prevented them from being known to anyone outside the immediate family. It is only very recently that their significance as important historical and social documents has become recognised.

A Tour of Ireland through the eyes of Lord Mark Kerr

Ballycastle. View in the Co. of Antrim, Kinban Head   1833

ANNE CASEMENT
with contributions from
HECTOR McDONNELL
TOM McNEILL
ANNESLEY MALLEY
IAN MONTGOMERY
FRED HAMOND
MALACHY McSPARRAN
ALEX BLAIR

Detail from Map of Ireland for *Lewis's Atlas of Ireland*, 1837

Donaghadee																													17 NOVEMBER 1809

DONAGHADEE

This port on the County Down coast was the Irish terminal of the packet boat, the ferry from Portpatrick, which was the best means of reaching the north of Ireland from Britain. It was the route used by the Kerrs on all their visits to Ireland, apart from the first one, in 1802, when they took the packet boat from Holyhead in Anglesea to Dunleary as on that occasion they were going to Dublin. In those pre-railway days it would have been necessary for the Kerr family to make the entire overland journey from their home in the south of England in their carriage, which would then have been loaded onto the ferry at Portpatrick, and offloaded in Donaghadee so that they could continue to their destinations in Ireland. The carriage shown in this drawing may well be therefore a depiction of the Kerrs' own vehicle. Mark Kerr seems to have had a particular affection for his carriages, which he drew on several occasions. He often amused his children by telling ridiculous stories about adventures which had befallen him during carriage rides.

Inevitably travel was a long and tiring business, requiring many breaks, and this in part explains why the Kerrs frequently stayed with the Londonderry family at Mount Stewart at the beginning and end of their Irish visits. Mount Stewart was only a few miles from Donaghadee, and the sea voyage was often the most disagreeable part of their journeys. Mark Kerr produced several drawings while they were waiting for the right conditions to sail, including one 'Monster Drawing' entitled 'The Paquet Bird going with fair wind to Donaghadee'.

Two paddle steamers, *Dasher* and *Arrow*, were sent from Dover to take over this route in 1825, thus greatly improving the speed and comfort of the crossing.

Garron Point   AUGUST 1838

Garron Point, Turnly's Pass   1839

ANTRIM COAST ROAD

For many years the Antrim Coast Road was believed to have been a famine relief project, but it is now clear that it was built between 1832 and 1842. At that time, it was the biggest civil engineering scheme attempted in Ireland, and it is hard to appreciate today how eagerly awaited and advantageous an enterprise the new road must have been. Prior to its construction access to the Antrim coast was easier by sea than by land as the existing road could not pass around the many headlands along its route, but was forced to ascend and descend each in turn. Despite these difficulties, by the early nineteenth century a steadily increasing number of tourists was using the coast road to gain access to the Giant's Causeway.

Mc Donnell's Pass
20 AUGUST

Two headlands, in particular, were notoriously difficult, and carriages attempting to traverse them required the help of additional horses, stabled beside the road for the purpose. One of these was the fearfully steep ascent and descent of Park Head, immediately east of Glenarm. A line for the proposed new road, approaching the headland across an area of ground formerly used by Lord Antrim as a deer park, had been suggested as early as 1820, but construction was not completed until about 1835. It probably involved blasting back the chalk headland to create a platform wide enough to accommodate the road, and high enough to prevent it being washed away. In his August 20th sketch, Mark Kerr shows the newly constructed road skirting a headland, and in other sketches he shows the techniques employed in its construction.

In 1839 Mark Kerr did a painting of Turnly's Pass – a pass cut through the limestone rock near Garron Point in 1822 to attempt to ease the descent at this, the second notably difficult headland. Previously it had been negotiated via the precipitous Foaran (i.e. cold) Path, so-called because at its base it crossed the icy waters of a stream renowned as the shortest river in Ireland, being all of one hundred yards in length. The work was the inspiration of a local landowner, Francis Turnly, who owned property at both Cushendall and Drumnasole, south of Garron Point, and wished to make commuting between the two less arduous. Mark Kerr, too, would have benefited from Turnly's munificence as he and his family made their way north towards Ballycastle, and their journeys to and from Glenarm were to be transformed by the subsequent creation of the Antrim Coast Road.

Garron Point Pass cut through the Solid Lime Stone Cliff
11 OCTOBER 1828

The Maidens from the Shore Road　　　　　　　　　　　　　　　　　　　　　　　　　　　　　　　　　　8 OCTOBER 1835

MAIDENS LIGHTHOUSES

The strong tides and rocky shoreline of the North Channel are extremely hazardous for sailors and shipping, and several lighthouses have been erected to guide them, and warn of impending dangers. A pair of lighthouses on the Maidens Rocks came into operation in 1829. Both were manned and had accommodation for the keeper and his family. No one was better placed than Mark Kerr to appreciate the benefit of such facilities, which for him must have provided one of the most striking and novel examples of the technological capabilities of the age in which he lived, and the march of progress in the previously largely undeveloped and inaccessible Glens of Antrim.

The 84-feet high (25m) west light was abandoned in 1903, and the buildings have now been taken over by seabirds as prime nest sites. The remaining 94-feet high (29m) east light is visible for about 23 miles. All lighthouses and lightships around the Irish coast are now administered by the Commissioners of Irish Lights, which were established in 1867. The east light was automated in 1977 and is now controlled centrally from Dublin.

Glenarm Castle from the Park   1809

GLENARM CASTLE FROM THE PARK

This drawing commemorates the Kerrs' first sight of Charlotte's family's country seat, now the home of her elder sister, Anne Catherine, and her first husband, Sir Harry Vane-Tempest. Because of the vicious legal dispute over the Antrim inheritance the Kerrs were on extremely bad terms with Anne Catherine and Harry Vane-Tempest, so it is probable that they would not have visited the family home at all at this time, and that this drawing represents the only view they had of the property as they passed by on their way to and from the house they stayed in at Ballycastle. The drawing was probably done from near the coast road, which at this stage still went over Park Head to the east of Glenarm.

The original house had been completed in 1636 by the 1st Earl of Antrim, but this was burnt in 1642 by an invading Covenanting army under Monro and had stood as a roofless shell until it was restored in the Palladian style in the 1750s. The doorway and windows of the house were subsequently gothicised by Sir Harry, who also added a small Gothic wing onto the eastern side; but it appears that at the time of this drawing this transformation had not yet begun.

The drawing also shows Glenarm Parish Church, built in 1763, possibly to designs by the British architect and civil engineer, Christopher Myers, who came from Whitehaven, and may also have been the architect of the Palladian castle. The church includes a clock made in Whitehaven in 1759, and a bell dated 1758, both of which were presented by Sir Harry in 1806. They most likely came from a building adjacent to the castle which he had demolished.

Glenarm – in a confounded hurry   MARCH 1826

BATTLEMENTS, GLENARM CASTLE

In 1826, Mark Kerr drew this scene 'in a confounded hurry' from the garden of the agent's house at the top of Altmore Street in Glenarm village, on the opposite side of the Glenarm river to the castle. At the time of the Kerrs' visit, it was probably occupied by Thomas Davison and had acquired its present handsome Georgian fanlighted doorway, fronting the street. It seems that during this brief first visit to Glenarm the Kerrs lodged here rather than the castle, as Charlotte still could not bring herself to stay with her sister, despite the fact that Mark Kerr and Anne Catherine's second husband, Edmund McDonnell, had already made friends, and an open invitation to the Kerrs had been extended some years before.

In the mid-1820s Anne Catherine and Edmund had commissioned the renowned Irish architect, William Vitruvius Morrison, to transform the existing house at Glenarm into a Jacobethan castle. Mark Kerr's drawing shows the great battlemented range of walls and towers which had been created along the riverbank, and the new gatehouse which now formed the entrance to the castle. The tower on the battlements to the left of this entranceway housed a lavatory, the castle's first sanitary installation. Proper plumbing did not arrive for another generation, though running cold water was piped to the kitchens as part of the Morrison scheme.

The Ladye's Tower. Glenarm Castle   28 AUGUST

Entrance to Glenarm Castle											1828

BARBICAN BRIDGE ENTRANCE TO GLENARM CASTLE

This is one of the drawings done by Mark Kerr during his family's first visit to Glenarm Castle in 1828, which marked the healing of the rift between Anne Catherine and Charlotte. It was highly unusual for him to depict human activity in his topographical drawings, and when he did so it almost invariably consisted of rather vague representations of his own children. It may, therefore, not be too fanciful to suggest that the carriage seen crossing the bridge to enter the castle grounds in this drawing is supposed to represent, or at least commemorate, his family's first stay in Charlotte's ancestral home. She herself had not visited it since she was as a teenager, over thirty years before.

The barbican gatehouse had been completed in 1825, so it was very new at the time of the Kerrs' visit, but the bridge itself was over a hundred years old. The coast road, and therefore all public traffic, had passed over it until the road was diverted over a new bridge nearer to the sea in 1823. Edmund McDonnell had met some of the cost of constructing this new bridge, discernible in the background of Mark Kerr's picture, which enabled the old one to be solely used by visitors to the castle.

BARBICAN GATE, GLENARM CASTLE

Having entered the castle, the Kerrs would have been able to pause and properly appreciate the gatehouse, which was the centrepiece of the battlemented wall built along the river to designs by William Vitruvius Morrison. His drawings for the barbican reveal that the finished structure differed somewhat from that envisaged by him. Mark Kerr depicts the inner face of the building very accurately, including the plaque commemorating its commissioning by Edmund and Anne Catherine.

Pseudo-medieval entrance gatehouses were a particular speciality of William Vitruvius and his father, Richard. The first of these, designed by Richard Morrison, was built in 1812, at Thomastown Castle, County Tipperary, while a year later one was built at Borris House, County Carlow. Both Morrisons worked at Borris, but it is likely that the gatehouse must have been designed by William Vitruvius as it follows a very similar pattern to Glenarm, with a small lodge for a gatekeeper on one side, and a tower on the opposite side containing a spiral staircase leading to the upper levels of the gatehouse. The Borris gatehouse has a strongly medieval feel to it, however, as has William Vitruvius's Brittas Castle gatehouse of 1834, whereas the Glenarm barbican is more Elizabethan. A coat of arms of 1636, commemorating the completion of the original castle, was incorporated into the entrance front of the Glenarm gatehouse to give extra credence to its air of antiquity.

The Barbican at Glenarm   27 AUGUST 1828

Glenarm Castle S. & W. Fronts

OCTOBER 1828

GLENARM CASTLE

This drawing was also done on the Kerrs' first visit to the castle, and highlights the fact that, for reasons which remain unclear, the conversion of the Palladian house into a Jacobethan castle appears to have been carried out in two phases. Mark Kerr's drawing shows the house at an uncomfortable stage of this transformation. The cornice, pediment and upper triple windows of the Palladian house are still intact, as are the Gothic windows and doorway inserted by Harry Vane-Tempest in the early 1800s, but by the mid-1820s these had been neatly, if incongruously, sandwiched between four pepperpot towers, designed by William Vitruvius Morrison. Immediately to the right of the main block is the small Gothic wing added by Harry Vane-Tempest to house a billiard room on the lower floor and an extra bedroom above, both lit by Regency Gothic bay windows. Beyond is one range of the east wing designed by Morrison to accommodate the inside staff. The ground floor of this range housed the still room and housekeeper's parlour, while above were the bedrooms for female servants, the door to them being kept locked at night to deter male visitors. The windows of these rooms were above head height, so as to prevent staff spying on the family and their guests enjoying themselves in the castle grounds.

Mark Kerr's drawing is the most complete image known of the south and west fronts during this curious intermediary phase before the transformation of the house into a Jacobethan castle was completed by changes to the roofscape and fenestration, and the addition of an Elizabethan entrance porch, which occurred in the early 1840s, under the superintendence of the architect Charles Lanyon.

Corner of the Offices, Glenarm Castle
SEPTEMBER 1828

EAST WING, GLENARM CASTLE

William Vitruvius Morrison's east wing, depicted here, contained carefully designed servants' quarters. The tower in the middle housed a staircase leading to the head cook's bedroom and a well-aired game larder at the top. To the left of it, on the ground floor, were a large scullery and an ingenious feather loft, feathers being in constant demand in a big house for use in upholstery and bedding. On the ground floor to the right were another scullery and vegetable store. Beyond lay the servants' hall and staircase to bedrooms for the male staff. The balustraded steps at the left-hand end led up to the front of the castle.

Offices at Glenarm Castle
28 AUGUST 1828

COTTAGE, GLENARM PARK

Deerpark Cottage, as this hunting lodge in the cottage orné style was generally called, was situated in the middle of the deer park, about two miles up the glen from the castle, and was used by the family and their guests whilst out hunting deer, fishing in the nearby river, or on excursions through the park. Such hunting lodges were a normal part of the arrangements provided for the entertainment of family and guests on a typical country estate. Mark Kerr was a keen sportsman and must have made this drawing during one of his hunting expeditions at Glenarm.

Cottage in Glenarm Park

The cottage would have been only a few years old at the time of the 1828 drawing, as it was most probably one of the many improvements Edmund McDonnell made to the estate. It contained a small sitting-room and dining-room, and several bedrooms. Nearby were a couple of small dwellings for domestic staff, together with gardens and a coach house. It was thus a miniature, self-contained place of country pleasures.

Cottage in Glenarm Park
OCTOBER 1828

Letitia, Marchioness of Antrim's Cottage – with a small fall on the River. Glenarm Park 1828

LETITIA, MARCHIONESS OF ANTRIM'S COTTAGE, GLENARM PARK

Letitia, Marchioness of Antrim, was Mark Kerr's mother-in-law. She was married firstly, at the age of thirteen, to Lord Dungannon's son and heir. The bridegroom was understood to be simple-minded, and it is said she was young and naïve enough to have agreed to the match by the promise of a diamond hoop. A year later she gave birth to a son, Arthur Hill-Trevor, who would become Anne Catherine's and Charlotte's half-brother, and by the age of twenty-one she was a widow. In 1774 she married Randal William McDonnell, who became the 6th Earl and later Marquis of Antrim. He died in 1791, so this cottage was probably built in the 1770s or 1780s, and is the earliest ornamental park building at Glenarm for which there is any visual record.

It stood in the deerpark, a little further away from the castle than the Deerpark Cottage. Its life was relatively short as Letitia Louisa's caption to Mark Kerr's sketch indicates that it was in poor condition, and by 1847 it had become so dilapidated it was pulled down. The ten-foot-high walls which enclosed the courtyard behind it are still partly intact today.

In Glenarm River   OCTOBER 1828

BRIDGE, GLENARM RIVER

Mark Kerr was clearly impressed by these elegant old bridges which spanned the river in the deerpark and provided crossings for the horsemen who would have hunted the deer in the three-thousand-acre park. They were probably built c. 1750–60 when Glenarm was developed as the country seat of the Antrim family. In the nineteenth century the advent of the modern rifle resulted in stalking replacing riding to hounds as the preferred method of hunting deer, and one characteristic use of these bridges thus ceased.

BULL'S EYE WATERFALL, GLENARM PARK

The Bull's Eye is the grandest of the waterfalls on the Glenarm river, and also the most distant from the castle. To reach it required an expedition of about four miles through the deerpark; nonetheless it seems to have been a favourite destination for guests staying at the castle. The Bull's Eye was frequently painted by members of the family, often with a fisherman working his rod and line in the water below, which was an exciting and profitable place to fish as the fall prevented the progress of salmon further up the river.

The drawing masters employed by the family seem to have enjoyed trying to get their pupils to produce suitably romantic landscape studies including this natural feature. One of these, done by Anne Catherine, proudly bears the inscription 'Lady Antrim's first watercolour'. It is an intensely worked piece, and was subsequently acquired by Charlotte, herself a good water-colourist with a propensity for romantic landscapes. It is thus easy to understand why Mark Kerr felt the need to try his hand at depicting the Bull's Eye, though it was in fact the only time that he attempted to represent such a scene.

Fall in Glenarm Park 42 feet called Bull's Eye — OCTOBER 1828

Fall in the River at Glenarm — 1839

Between Nappan and Glenarm
1835

NAPPAN

Nappan would have been one of the first landmarks on the Kerrs' journey northwards from Glenarm. It lay at the northern end of the plateau between Carnlough and Garron Point, known as the Largy, meaning the side or slope of a hill. The route of the original coast road lay across the Largy, and Mark Kerr's 1835 drawing clearly shows the line of this road, known as the Largy road, snaking its way across the plateau.

A strong rivalry existed between the Kerrs and Frances Anne Vane-Tempest, Anne Catherine's only child. She had inherited valuable estates in County Durham from her father, Sir Harry Vane-Tempest, and was the wife of a substantial Ulster landlord, Lord Londonderry. The Kerrs' means, by comparison, were distinctly modest. For her part, Frances Anne felt slighted by the fact that, because she was a woman, Charlotte's and Mark's sons would inherit the Antrim title in preference to herself. In 1848, she determined to stamp her mark on the Antrim lands she had acquired upon the death of her mother by building a fine residence there. Garron Tower, as the house was called, was officially opened in 1850 by Lord Clarendon, the Lord Lieutenant of Ireland, and was a splendid castellated affair, perched on the cliff top at Garron Point. The demesne surrounding the house comprised some of the finest land on her estate. It was entered through a gilded pair of wrought-iron gates, set in the estate wall, and the area within included fine gardens and pleasure grounds. To achieve this effect, Frances Anne was forced to alter the line of the Largy road to a new course tucked under the hillside to the west. Nonetheless, its original route may still be observed within the fields of Nappan and grounds of Garron Tower.

COAST GUARD STATION, GARRON POINT

The Antrim Plateau commands fine views of the North Channel and thus provides the perfect location for observing the movement of boats, including those used by smugglers. Smuggling flourished along this coast in the eighteenth and early nineteenth centuries, and was one of the reasons behind the establishment of the Coastguard Force in 1822. Several coastguard stations were erected along the east Antrim coast, each comprising a watch house, boat house and basic single-storey cottage for the officer and boatmen. Mark Kerr made two drawings of the station on Garron Point, and it is easy to appreciate its attraction for a man whose working life had been spent in the Navy. His interest and understanding of his subject are demonstrated by the way he clearly illustrates the flagstaff, complete with yardarm, for it was by means of flags that neighbouring stations kept in contact with each other, and relayed information about naval traffic. He also shows a window in the seaward gable of the watchhouse, presumably the vantage point of the watchman.

Coastguard personnel were later accommodated in cottages enjoying a more sheltered location on the shore below.

Pass cut through the Chalk Cliff Garron Point   1828

Coast Guard Station Garron Point

4 OCTOBER

GLENARIFF

The dramatic, steeply sloping sides of Glenariff would have been sure to capture Mark Kerr's attention. In 1815 he drew the view up the glen from the north-eastern end of Red Bay. Accounts of the period hold conflicting views on its productivity, one observing that crops ripened earlier on its north-facing slopes than its south-facing ones, due to the fact that the latter were shaded from the sun in autumn by the high slopes of Luriegethan. Another stated that 'the Layd or north side is much more productive and better soil than that of Ardclinis, which is owing in a great measure to its being so much more exposed to the influence of the sun'. The glen was formerly densely wooded, but the expansion in the population from the mid-eighteenth century onwards, coupled with the difficulties experienced in obtaining a supply of fuel in this locality, led to the dramatic deforestation depicted by Mark Kerr. The area of dunes to the rear of the beach was known as the Warren, on account of its use as a source of rabbit meat and fur, but in former times potatoes planted in seaweed had been cultivated here. Mark Kerr's drawing includes the two elliptical arches of the bridge over the Glenariff River, which was then only in 'middling order'.

Glenariff Bay provided a safe anchorage in all but an easterly wind, and fishing formed a significant part of the local economy. There was a salmon fishery in the mouth of the Glenariff river, which captured fish returning to spawn in the waters of their birth; and cod, mackerel, herring and flat fish, as well as lobsters and crabs, were plentiful in the bay. Both drift and draft nets were used for herring fishing, and at dusk hundreds of men, women and children, known as carpers, congregated on the beach to catch the fish that broke from the draft net as it was hauled ashore.

Glenariffe 1815

RED BAY ARCH

The Kerrs' journey northwards in 1826 would have enabled them, for the first time, to avoid the extremely steep, twisty and narrow track which previously was the only means of negotiating Crookanavick headland at the northern end of Red Bay, in favour of a new route around the point created by Francis Turnly in 1817, again to ease his journey between his estates at Cushendall and Drumnasole. Mark Kerr was suitably impressed, and drew the fine arch that Turnly blasted through the headland to provide a route for the new road. A large cave is understood to have once existed beneath Red Bay Castle, and it may have formed an obvious line of construction for the new road, as no cave of similar dimensions exists today.

Pass Red Bay Castle

MARCH 1826

20

Cave Cottage in the County of Antrim. MRK 1819.

RED BAY CAVES

Smaller caves do still remain at Red Bay, which have enjoyed a colourful and chequered history. In Mark Kerr's time, two were used either as a forge or to store fishing nets. Kerr depicts another, 'Nanny's Cave', which had been transformed into a dwelling by walling up the entrance with stones. Its two rooms were home to Ann Murray, who supplemented a meagre income from knitting and spinning by selling whiskey illegally. She tried to evade the licensing laws by claiming that the spring in her cave had miraculous properties and she was merely selling spring water, giving *poitin* free with each glass. Nonetheless she was twice imprisoned but saved on both occasions by the intervention of an influential gentleman. She survived in this damp and gloomy spot for fifty years, in conditions which would have taxed the strongest of constitutions, and yet she lived on until 1847, dying, it is said, aged one hundred years. Mark Kerr was a firm believer in the restorative powers of *poitin*, sending for supplies when his gout was at its most troublesome, and might have attributed Nanny's longevity to regular doses of her own medicine.

One of these caves during Penal Times had functioned as a school for Catholic children, and could number amongst its former pupils, James McDonnell, later Dr James McDonnell, 'the father of Belfast medicine' and co-founder of the Belfast Dispensary and Fever Hospital, the direct ancestor of the Royal Victoria Hospital. The breadth of his interests was extraordinary, ranging from medicine and geology to Irish republicanism and culture. Dr James was a distant relation of Charlotte's, and much admired in the family, particularly for his championing of Irish harpists.

Mark Kerr was delighted to learn it was McDonnell who had intervened on Ann Murray's behalf.

Cave Cottage
Red Bay

Remains of Red Bay Castle   7 SEPTEMBER 1838

RED BAY CASTLE

Kerr depicts the view from the north-west looking towards Garron Point, with fragments of masonry perched on a mound. This viewpoint shows to best advantage the ditch and mound, which may be the motte of a castle of c. 1200. The standing masonry is all that remained in his day of a stone castle, possibly built in the later sixteenth century. Mark Kerr shows fragments of a tower, complete with a section of moulded corbelled string course in the Scottish style, and part of the adjoining curtain wall. The south-east angle and about half of the east wall of the tower survive today. Kerr's view shows the tower wall as the most prominent piece of masonry. He represents the tower, however, as a wall stretching to the left and right of an exterior angle towards the right-hand end. In fact this is the reverse of the true situation. It is the inner face of the wall which is observable from the position Kerr made his drawing, with the interior angle to the right. It would seem as though he made a hasty sketch of the monument in the field, marking the interior angle with a vertical line. When he came to ink the field sketch up, he mistook this line for the line of an exterior angle and drew the rest of the tower to fit, running it into the line of the curtain wall to the east and north.

Joined to the left of the tower is a low fragment of the curtain wall surrounding a courtyard which adjoined the castle to the south. To the right are two fragments of masonry which by virtue of their position must be fragments of the south-western section of the curtain wall. These are now no more than foundations in the grass, but a photograph published in 1952 shows a pile of tumbled stonework in this location, as though such a wall as Kerr portrays had just collapsed.

Cushendall   27 SEPTEMBER 1833

CUSHENDALL

Mark Kerr was a major landowner in the parish of Layd, in which Cushendall was situated. He appears to have sketched this view of the village from the former route of the coast road, known as the stoney loanin, some distance before it descended into the village itself.

By 1833, when the sketch was made, the village had been in the possession of Francis Turnly for twenty years. As a young man, Turnly had gone out to China, returning in 1801 having amassed a considerable fortune, which he used to purchase estates at Cushendall and Drumnasole. He was by all accounts eccentric, if not mad, and devised many grandiose schemes for improving his Cushendall estate. His most lasting memorial is Turnly's Tower, clearly visible in the centre of this drawing, which may have been constructed from stone resulting from the blasting out of the Red Arch. It seems likely that its primary function was as a folly or eyecatcher, though in this case unusually situated in an urban rather than rural setting, but it subsequently accommodated a spring-fed reservoir feeding a fountain on the east wall. Turnly appears to have had another use entirely in mind for the building – that of a prison. He appointed an army pensioner to guard it, and stipulated that it was to be provisioned for a year and armed with a musket, bayonet, case of pistols and pike thirteen feet long, with a cross on its handle to prevent it being pulled through the hole guarding the doorway. The bell within the tower was to be rung nightly at nine, and at no other time, except in an emergency.

Turnly was, nonetheless, aware of the village's potential as a tourist resort, and completed its first hotel, The Glens of Antrim, as it became known, convenient to the beach. The gabled end of the uppermost building in the drawing is probably 'The Cottage', which he seems to have built to serve as holiday accommodation for female members of his family.

Cary Castle   OCTOBER 1833

CASTLE CARRA, CUSHENDUN

Kerr's drawings of Castle Carra were done in 1833 during the final, nostalgic tour of Antrim he and Charlotte made before her death. It formed a fitting part of such an itinerary, having been immortalized in MacDonnell folklore as the place where in 1567 they avenged the defeat inflicted upon them by Shane O'Neill at the battle of Glentaisie, by slaughtering Shane and his followers in a drunken brawl. The records merely state that Shane died 'in his camp', but nonetheless a tradition grew up that his death took place at Castle Carra. Kerr draws the north-east and south-east sides of the castle, clearly showing its sloping base and the only original surviving doorway, to the right-hand-side, which was reached via external stairs leading up to an entrance platform.

The castle structure was at least two hundred years old when Shane was killed, and was probably associated with adjacent domestic accommodation. It was subsequently used as a smithy, and Mark Kerr may have been aware of its use as a killeen for the burial of unbaptised or stillborn infants.

9 OCTOBER 1833

CASTLE CARRA AND VIEW TO SOUTH-WEST

In this drawing Mark Kerr heightens the historical allusion by including the unmistakable silhouette of Tievebulliagh in his composition. Here we have a place whose significance stretches as far back as the Neolithic period. Outcrops of porcellanite, an extremely hard and tough rock, ideal for the manufacture of axe heads, occur here, one of only two such outcrops in County Antrim. Neolithic people were naturally attracted by such material, and established an axe-factory on the mountainside, where the rock was extracted and roughly chipped into axe or adze blades. These 'rough-outs' then seem to have been carried away for finishing elsewhere by grinding and polishing. Porcellanite is such a rare and distinctive material that it is almost certain that any blade found in the British Isles came from a County Antrim source. Mark Kerr also had a personal interest in Tievebulliagh as it lay within Charlotte's estate. He had ordered the creation of a new road there to facilitate the transport of chalk, which was burnt in kilns to produce lime for use as a fertilizer or for building purposes.

Framed by the plantation between the castle and Tievebulliagh appears to be the cluster of buildings surrounding the Ballindam corn mill at Mill Town. Water to drive this mill was stored in a dam above it. In dry weather this sometimes proved insufficient, and may explain why the mill probably became redundant following the erection of a fine new one nearby at Whitehouse in 1847. The neighbouring plantation was a major feature of the park surrounding Cushendun House, the earliest house built by the gentry to enjoy the attractive seaside location of Cushendun. From its windows there were delightful views over the entire length of Cushendun Bay. It belonged to the McNeill family, but the incumbent in Mark Kerr's day was Edmund Alexander McNeill, whose wife Rose seems to have preferred warmer and more sociable environments than those of Cushendun, and from the early 1830s the house was seldom occupied. It was accidentally destroyed by fire in 1928.

Cushendun Rocks

6 SEPTEMBER 1811

CUSHENDUN

Mark Kerr's curiosity was obviously aroused by the texture of the rocks at the southern end of Cushendun Bay, which are puddingstones, or more correctly conglomerates, here consisting of a hardened mixture of water-worn cobbles in a matrix of sand. The sea has created caves within these rocks, which are amongst the greatest, but least known, geological wonders of Ulster. In Mark Kerr's day the interiors of these caves were used as a powder magazine, cow house, smith's forge and store rooms.

The entranceways for pedestrians and carriages on the right of the drawing entitled 'Cushendun – near the caves', led up to an isolated cottage, picturesquely enclosed by high cliffs on three sides and the sea on the other. It was the property of Nicholas Delacherois Crommelin, 'an expansive and expensive gentleman', who had acquired a lease of an extensive tract of barren upland between Cushendun and Ballymena from Sir Harry Vane-Tempest in 1800. He conceived several, mostly spectacularly unsuccessful, schemes for improving this area, including the establishment of a new settlement and mining community, named Newtown-Crommelin, and the creation of a harbour at Cushendun, in the area depicted by Mark Kerr, to serve both Newtown-Crommelin and Ballymena. Newtown-Crommelin enjoyed but limited success before its rapid decline, and, despite an Act of Parliament of 1830 'for establishing and maintaining the harbour of Port Crommelin', no finance could be secured for the scheme. Its construction would have involved the destruction of the caves.

Cushendun – near the caves

26

Clare and the coast from Dunaneeny Castle
18 OCTOBER 1828

CLARE PARK, BALLYCASTLE

On visits to Lady Charlotte's unmarried agent Edmund McGildowney, the Kerrs stayed with his elder brother, Charles, and his wife, at Clare Park, which enjoyed a picturesque, but very exposed, location on the cliff-top just west of Ballycastle. Charles, himself, was Lady Charlotte's seneschal for Ballymoney.

The house was neat but rather small, with nothing remarkable in its appearance. It was subsequently extended and made more fanciful and romantic by the addition of features such as oriel windows and a tower. The upstairs rooms overlooking the sea enjoyed tremendous views across the Straits of Moyle. It was demolished, piecemeal, in the last years of the twentieth century and early years of the twenty-first.

Due east of Clare Park lie the remains of Dunineny Castle. Dunineny, or the 'fort of the fair', is understood to have been the original setting for a fair which was the forerunner of Ballycastle's famous Lammas Fair. In the foreground of this sketch is the ditch (much overemphasised by Mark Kerr) dug to cut off the promontory on which Dunineny Castle was sited from the adjacent land. Midway along this ditch are the remains of a seventeenth-century stone building resembling a gate house, and within the enclosure lay at least two substantial timber-framed structures. Castles traditionally have a combination of military, residential and administrative roles. Defensively Dunineny was a sham as the gatehouse had no back wall, and there was no curtain wall or bank. Nor is there any evidence to suggest that the buildings were ever used by the McDonnells as a residence. Their prime function appears to have been as an administrative centre for the barony.

Clare 17 MARCH 1826

Bally Castle

BALLYCASTLE

Mark Kerr here depicts all that remained in his day of a castle thought to have been constructed in Ballycastle in the first half of the seventeenth century by one of the 1st Earl of Antrim's important local tenants, Hugh McNeill. It was similar to other turreted tower houses in the Scottish style built at the same time on the Antrim estate, such as Ballygalley Castle. Randal Arranagh, the 1st Earl of Antrim, was a shrewd operator, and cleverly provided accommodation for himself and his family in this part of his huge estate by requiring a right of residence in McNeill's castle whenever he wished to stay. Its site was in the central area of Ballycastle, known as the Diamond. It lay beside the steep bank of a stream, and commanded a fine view towards the coast and into Glentaisie. The town itself was laid out, not in the haphazard Irish way, but as neat houses on either side of a main street, which widened at one end into a market-place or Diamond. This was the model for many towns created following the Plantation of Ulster in the seventeenth century, the market end of the main street being generally enclosed by the Plantation castle.

Part of the fabric of the castle is said to have been removed to permit the construction of Holy Trinity Church in the Diamond, in 1756. Dwellings had also been built right beside it. The last vestiges were demolished about 1856.

21 AUGUST 1811

Bally Castle – Fairhead – Coast of Scotland

In the mid-eighteenth century, under the aegis of Hugh Boyd, Ballycastle underwent a remarkable period of development and became, albeit briefly, one of the foremost industrialized towns in Ireland. Hugh Boyd was the son of the rector of Ramoan and his wife Rose McNeill, who had acquired the McNeill estate, which included much of the land around Ballycastle. Hugh himself purchased the town of Ballycastle from the 5th Earl of Antrim in 1727. Prior to this he had been a colliery manager there, and in 1735 he acquired the mining rights to its coalfield, which over the next twenty years he expanded and developed. In an effort to extend the markets for his coal, he vastly improved the harbour facilities of the town, and established a number of coal-dependent industries such as a brewery, soap-works, tannery and chandlery.

Around 1750, he moved his family into the new manor house on the sea front, in the heart of his industrial empire. Its location should have been an idyllic one, but views to Fair Head were interrupted by the towering glass house, inner dock of the harbour crammed with sailing ships, and waggon-way to the collieries; and the air would have been filled with the noxious fumes permeating from the adjacent tannery and soap-works. In 1784, the Rev William Hamilton remarked on old Mr Boyd who, not possessed of any considerable fortune, nor supported by powerful natural connections, nor endowed with any very superior talents, 'opened public roads, formed a harbour, built a town, established manufactures, and lived to see a wild and lawless country become populous, cultivated and civilized'. 'What would Ireland be, if every town and village in the country had a landlord like this?' Due to a combination of family and economic factors, the majority of Hugh Boyd's industries fell rapidly into decline after his death in 1765.

GLASS HOUSE, BALLYCASTLE

Perhaps the most prominent of Hugh Boyd's industrial buildings was the glass works built in 1755 on the Glass Island at the mouth of the river Margy. Its enormous brick flue, some ninety feet high, dominated the local landscape, and it was understood by the Ordnance Survey to be one of the largest buildings of its kind in the United Kingdom. Its main product was bottle glass. All output ceased in the 1760s, and the flue was demolished in the 1880s.

This view looking westwards towards the glass house shows clearly the size of its stack in comparison with the nearby two- and three-storey Customs House and inn. The Customs House was required due to the town's designation as a 'port of discharge' in 1731, and bore the arms of George II. The inn, a forerunner of the present Marine Hotel, was erected by Hugh Boyd in 1749. Mark Kerr also shows the line of North Street, devoid of all development except at its lower end, and the Margy Bridge, at the mouth of the river Margy, which was 132 feet long and had five spans. It was swept away in 1857, but subsequently rebuilt.

Bridge Glass House and Port na Greagh
1833

The Quay and Glass House Bally Castle   27 JULY 1809

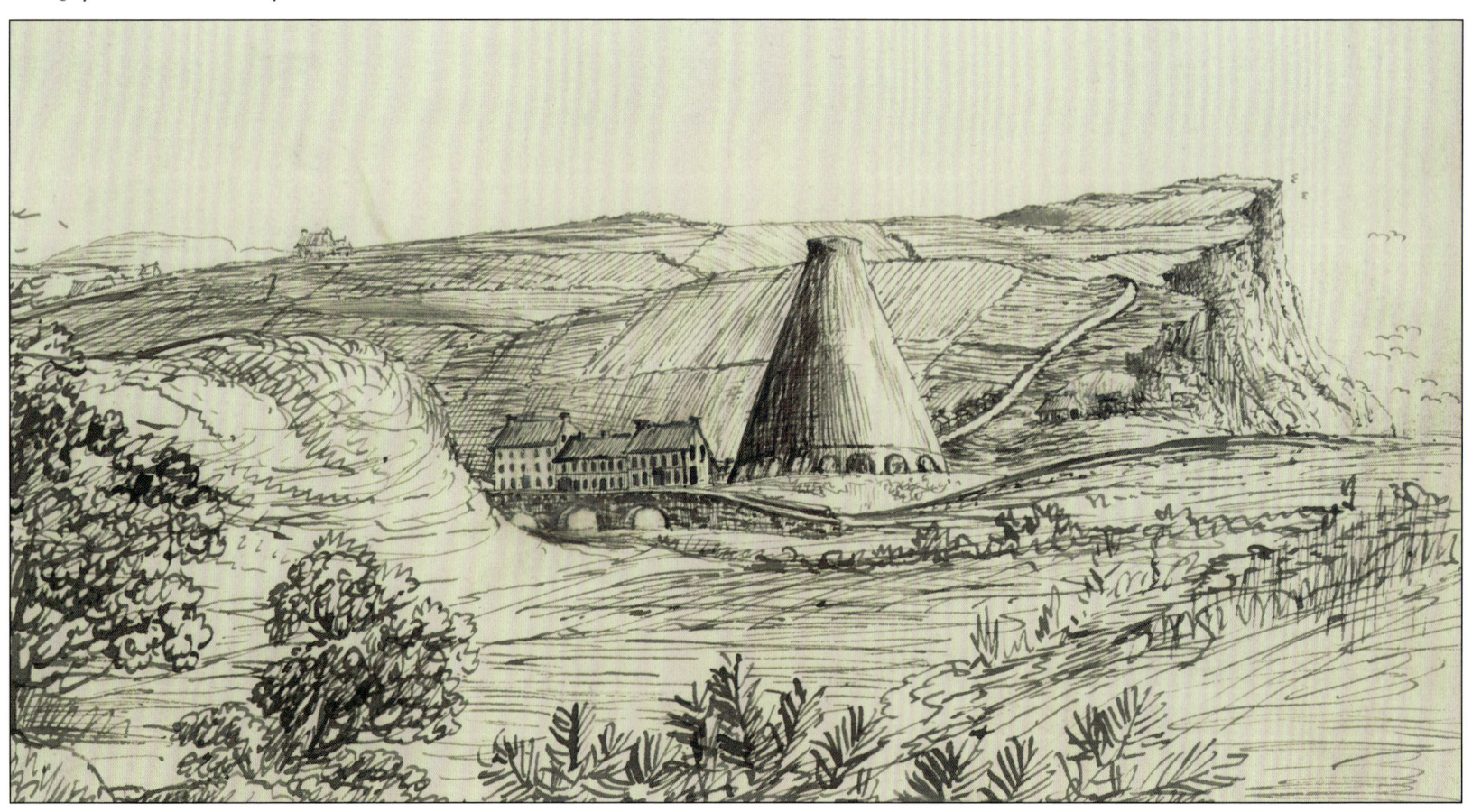

SOAP WORKS, BALLYCASTLE

Although Mark Kerr did not always record the scale and location of his subjects entirely faithfully, nonetheless an 1809 view seawards from the foot of Glentaisie towards Fair Head shows clearly the relationship between the octagonal spire of Holy Trinity church, the remaining gable-end of the McNeill castle, the glass house and a neighbouring dwelling, not the manor house, but possibly the former Sheskburn House, home of the Gage family of Rathlin. A short distance inland from the glass house is a long roofline and a rounded tower topped by a weather-vane. A closer view of the buildings near the seafront, drawn in 1815, shows this tower more distinctly, and reveals this to be the only known depiction of the huge chimney of the soap-works, which was octagonal in shape and used by the Boyd family as a flagstaff, a flag being raised whenever the family was in residence. This is clearly a subject which would have been of special appeal to a seaman such as Mark Kerr.

The Quay, Glass House and Island of Rathlin in the Distance. Ballycastle — 20 AUGUST 1815

Bally Castle from a byeroad above the Town — AUGUST 1809

Buonamargy Bally Castle   1809

BONAMARGY FRIARY, BALLYCASTLE

Bonamargy Friary was a small Franciscan friary, possibly founded in the fifteenth century. It was badly damaged in 1584, but was restored by Randal McDonnell, 1st Earl of Antrim, in the 1620s as a base for a Franciscan mission to the Western Isles of Scotland, which the Earl may have hoped would pave the way for a Catholic revival under his leadership of the ancient MacDonald Lordship of the Isles. His restoration consisted of rebuilding the upper parts and roofs of the church and north range, which provided a residence for the friars, and adding a south range to form a burial chapel for his family, and a gatehouse. Unlike the traditional plan of a medieval monastic house, the cloister at Bonamargy has only two sides, formed by the north wall of the church and west wall of the domestic range. As many as eight or nine friars may have been in residence at one time, one of whom would have been the prior. The church ceased to be a place of worship after the collapse of the west wall in the later eighteenth century, but the site continued to be used for burials.

The main difference between the building as seen by Mark Kerr and the present one is the partial collapse of the north gable of the north range, and the erosion of the upper parts of its east and west walls. The south range was also roofed when he saw it; the roof being removed later in the nineteenth century to make the ruin more romantic.

Buonamargy from the West   1 OCTOBER 1815

BONAMARGY FROM THE WEST

During his long stay in Ballycastle in 1815 Mark Kerr made a series of drawings of the friary. This view from the west shows the east window of the church, and the tall, arched doorway leading into the Antrim family chapel to the south, beneath which lay the family burial vault. The residence of the friars lies to the north, reached via doors in the north wall of the chancel and cloister area. The first floor windows of the west wall of the north range are partially present, together with the two door openings from this range into the adjoining yard, the most northerly of which an 1838 account described as 'disfigured'. The tiny window above the southern door lit the staircase connecting the ground and upper floors of this range. The first floor was probably used as a dormitory and accommodation for the prior, and the ground floor as a refectory and service room. A projecting latrine was attached to the north wall.

The church is littered with the debris of the west wall, which is said to have collapsed about 1770 in a great storm. This was tidied away as part of the various restorations which have taken place over the last hundred years. At the west end is the strange, perforated, disc-headed cross which is said to mark the grave of Julia McQuillan, the 'Black Nun of Bonamargy', a native of Connaught, who lived a reclusive life here in the mid-seventeenth century. To her were attributed remarkable prophetic powers.

Buonamargy from the Sea   25 SEPTEMBER 1815

BONAMARGY FROM THE SEA

Kerr's view from the north-east shows the north gable of the north range prior to its partial collapse down to the level of the dormitory floor. He also shows a square-headed window in the ground floor of the north wall. This is now a mere shapeless hole. The dormitory window on the first floor and the door to the latrine extension to the north are also depicted; the first square-headed, the latter segmental. Observable, too, is the scar of the latrine projection and its first floor.

To the east lies the small seventeenth-century gatehouse, which would have controlled the access to the friary through a boundary bank, of which little remains. The ground floor was mainly occupied by the entrance passage, whilst above was a small room only high enough in the centre for the porter to stand upright.

Buonamargy towards the Sea

24 SEPTEMBER 1815

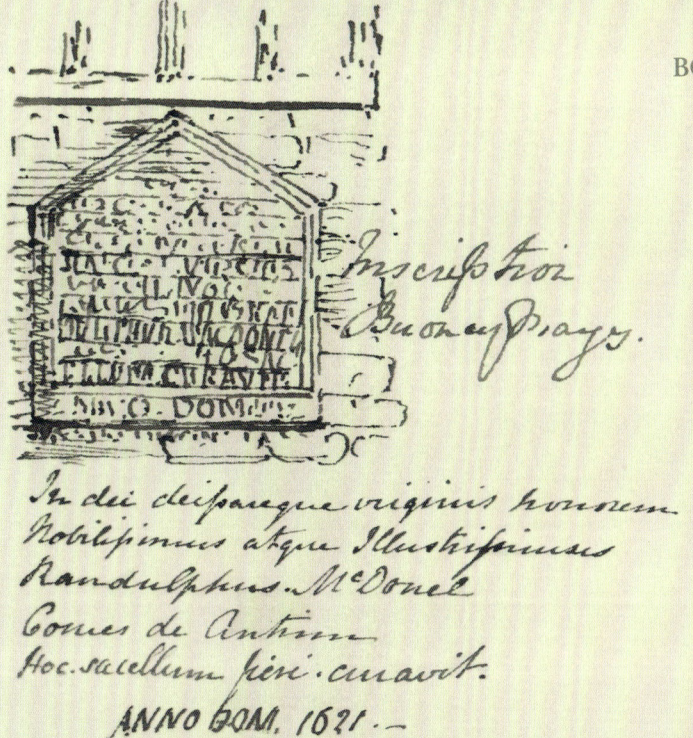

BONAMARGY TOWARDS THE SEA

The previous day Kerr had drawn the opposite south-eastern side of the friary showing the inside of the north gable of the north range, with the interior of the first floor window, and the south chapel still roofed. The attractive window in the south gable of the chapel is recorded as being closed up in 1838, and Kerr's drawing indicates this might have been the case in 1815. He depicts the panel beneath this window and was one of the few to record its Latin inscription, which by that time was almost illegible. This describes the construction of the chapel in 1621 by Randal McDonnell, the 1st Earl of Antrim. Kerr also shows the small stone cross which formerly surmounted the south gable.

The East Window of the Chapel
at Buonamargy

27 AUGUST 1815

Window at Buonamargy

WINDOWS AT BONAMARGY

This is a very fine representation of the exterior of the east window of the church, which was rebuilt as part of the restoration work carried out by the 1st Earl of Antrim. The outer carved stones are the remains of the terminals of the hood mould of the earlier window, decorated with stylised flat foliage carving. The detail of the carving on the south terminal is clearly shown in the sketch Kerr made of it below; this has since been affected by weathering. The three heads which mark the upper and lower extremities of the hood mould of the existing window are also clearly depicted.

He also drew two other windows within the friary. One is a fine view of the exterior of the south window of the church, though he has invented a relieving arch over the ogee-headed window. The other, of the east window in the ground floor in the north range, is somewhat strange. Presumably, the curious bowed jambs represent the way in which the window was accommodated into the curve of the barrel vault over the room.

Buonamargy

Bally Castle   2 AUGUST 1809

BALLYCASTLE FROM THE NORTH

One fine summer's afternoon Mark Kerr settled himself on the rising ground just north of the town to draw the spire of Holy Trinity church beneath him and the gables of the houses ascending Castle Street. Spread out before him was the rounded mass of Knocklayd, partly covered in trees, but elsewhere divided into neat rectangular fields. Such regular field patterns are commonplace today, but formerly much of the land in the glens had been subdivided into tiny, irregular units by farmers to provide for their children, or was held commonly by a group of farmers under the system of rundale. By the mid-nineteenth century such practices were actively discouraged by landowners and their agents, but proved extremely difficult to eradicate. In the glens they were generally replaced by the ladder farms which characterise the area, whereby each farmer got a fair share of the better and poorer land. This reorganisation is not thought to have become widespread until the years following the famine of the 1840s, but Kerr's drawings show that in north Antrim holdings had been divided into neat regular fields by the first years of the nineteenth century. This conclusion is borne out by the Reverend Richard Dobbs's 1817 statistical account of the neighbouring parishes of Ardclinis and Laid (Layd), which states that 'each person enjoys his own share exclusively, which encourages the making of fences'.

Fair Head from near Revd Hill's House

28 AUGUST 1815

BALLYCASTLE BAY

Mark Kerr here depicts the cluster of buildings at the east end of Ballycastle Bay, with Bath Lodge in the foreground, which is believed originally to have comprised the bath house for the collieries and adjoining manager's house. At the height of production in the 1750s, the mines employed over a hundred men, and it is easy to appreciate the need for such facilities. Production declined markedly following Hugh Boyd's death in 1765, and by Mark Kerr's time Bath Lodge had become the residence of the rector of Culfeightrin, the Reverend Hill. Mining nonetheless continued in a small way until the 1950s. Much of the output was for local consumption, but at times of peak production boats left Ballycastle carrying coal bound for destinations as far afield as the saltworks at Rostrevor, bleachworks around Belfast, and industrial concerns of Dublin.

The cluster of buildings on the left accommodated the salt works and Mark Kerr indicates the adjacent salt pans. In his day, salt was indispensable both as a seasoning and to preserve food. It was also used in the chemical industry, particularly in the production of bleach. Salt may be obtained from sea water, but in our climate natural evaporation is a slow and painstaking process, and far quicker results are achieved if heat is applied to drive off the unwanted water.

The presence of coal in a coastal situation such as Ballycastle made it an ideal place for salt production, and evaporation pans were located near the appropriately named 'Pans Rocks'. During the 1700s and early 1800s, a tax was levied on salt-making in Britain, which commonly involved the production of white-salt from rock-salt. Exports of rock-salt to Ireland were not taxed, however, and, as a result, there was a thriving production of white-salt manufactured in Ireland using rock-salt from Britain, some of which was illegally exported back to Britain. This was the process carried out at Ballycastle at the time of Mark Kerr's drawing, but he was witnessing the end of an era as production ceased just a few years later, due to the repeal of the salt tax.

Fair Head

20 AUGUST 1815

Bally Castle Colliery Houses 4 SEPTEMBER 1815

COLLIERY HOUSES, BALLYCASTLE

In 1815 Mark Kerr drew a group of colliery houses, possibly those shown surrounding the coal yard marked on the 1832 Ordnance Survey map in Ballyvoy townland west of Fair Head. His drawing appears to have been made from the side of the port known to have existed in this location, which lay beside a group of buildings which included a manager's house, cottages and workshops. Kerr also depicts material, presumably coal, which has been heaped up within the yard awaiting transportation.

Bally Castle Fair Head

FAIR HEAD

Mark Kerr was clearly fascinated by the magnificent columns that make up the face of Fair Head, which rises to a height of 636 feet above sea level. On one of his drawings he notes that 'one pillar is 306 feet high and more than 33 feet square more than the largest pillar either of nature or as in the known world'. His measurements are of the same order as those of the 1835 Ordnance Survey Memoir, which records the average size of the columns as 300 feet high and 20 feet square, the largest being roughly 40 feet in diameter.

Fair Head displays two examples of a sill, a geological sandwich in which the originally molten filling was squeezed between two existing layers of rock. As the filling cooled it contracted and cracked into the massive, crude columns that are clearly visible on the cliff face today. When weather conditions, particularly frost, penetrate these cracks, the columns collapse onto the huge area of boulder scree beneath. The fallen blocks comprising the scree are so large, heavy and resistant to the force of the sea that the scree has developed a stability unique around the shores of the British Isles.

Ruin of Culfeightrin　　　　　　　　　　　　　　　　　　　　　　　　　　　　　　31 AUGUST 1811

CULFEIGHTRIN CHURCH, GLENSHESK

This romantic ruin, according to Mark Kerr 'supposed to be the earliest building in this part of the country', lay on the site of a church, reputedly founded by Saint Patrick, situated on the Casement lands at Churchfield, south-east of Ballycastle. John Casement's connection to the McGildowney family presumably explains Kerr's knowledge of the site, where he sketched the view from the church towards the coast, and more especially, painstakingly recorded details of the fine Gothic tracery remaining in its east window. He seems to have had a Gaelic-speaking guide, who passed the time by regaling him with tales of Gobanseer, the legendary builder of the church. Gobanseer's life was threatened by the nobleman employing him, who feared Gobanseer might build fortresses for his rivals as strong as his own. Gobanseer engineered a stratagem whereby his wife might hold the nobleman's son hostage until Gobanseer was released. Beside his drawing, Kerr recorded their conversation, including attempts to transcribe his guide's Gaelic turn of phrase.

The remains of the church today comprise the east wall, a fragment of the south wall and the outline of the other walls, little different in fact to the ruin illustrated by Mark Kerr. The east window is a good example of a late medieval tracery design of the fourteenth or, more likely, the fifteenth century.

Bally Castle Co. Antrim

26 SEPTEMBER 1815

The wall stones are a geological mixture: some are derived from the neighbouring fields, but the window, for certain, is made from the fine-grained bed of sandstones exposed along the west face of Fair Head, also used for the finer carving at Bonamargy. The strong cusping which characterises its design remains very much as Kerr drew it; and he also shows the ivy-leaf carving on the terminals of the hood mould of the window. The curious lower arch caused the writer of the Ordnance Survey Memoir to attribute a crypt to the church, but it might simply be a relieving arch inserted because the east wall was built over uncertain foundations. Certainly the masonry below it shows no sign of being a later insertion. Mark Kerr has altered the proportions of the church, making it narrower than it is, and, consequentially, with a steeper pitch to the gable. He has also widened the view from the church and exaggerated the size of nearby buildings, such as the ruins of Bonamargy Abbey.

CROSS AT BROUGHANLEA

Mark Kerr appears to have been intrigued by the two strange symbols carved into a cross which he found about a mile east of Ballycastle, on the side of the road to Cushendall. The cross is thought to date from the fifth century, and reputedly was formerly located beside old Culfeightrin church, south-east of Ballycastle. An unwitting surveyor from the Ordnance Survey was informed that the motifs inscribed on the cross were smith's implements, namely a hammer and pinchers. It was suggested to him that at one time the cross was located beside a smith's forge, and the smith had probably inscribed the emblems on it 'for a public sign of his habitation and trade'. In reality, the two motifs are thought to be a bishop's crozier and Tau (t-shaped) cross. Tau crosses are rare, which may explain Kerr's interest in this one, the most well-known being that on Tory Island, off the Donegal coast.

The Tau cross, named after the Greek letter it resembles, is suspected to have originated with the Egyptians, and was of symbolic significance to many cultures before Christianity, being strongly identified with the bull. It has been a Christian symbol from the beginning, and is most commonly associated with St Francis of Assisi. In mythology it was the symbol of the Greek god Attis and Roman god Mithras, and their forerunner Tammuz, the Sumerian sun god, who was associated with fishing and shepherding. This may be of significance if, as suggested, the cross at Broughanlea once lay beside old Culfeightrin church, reputedly founded by the shepherd boy St Patrick.

Remains of an Ancient Cross, near Ballycastle. Aug.t 27.th 1815

Church Rathlin Island   1833

ST THOMAS'S CHURCH, RATHLIN ISLAND

Mark Kerr depicts the pretty little Church of Ireland church on the west side of Church Bay, Rathlin, which was apparently started in 1815, but not completed until 1823, just ten years before Kerr's sketch. It stands on the site of an early church built by St Comgall in the sixth century, which was destroyed in a Viking raid.

The building is plain and simple in design, constructed of random limestone blocks interspersed with a few basalt ones. The charming Gothic windows are filled with plain glass, including the one at the eastern end depicted here, which affords the congregation a wonderfully peaceful and contemplative view across Church Bay. The battlements encircling the tower give the building the look of a toy fort – a fashionable conceit of the time.

Within there is a particularly distinctive monument to a former rector, the Reverend John Martin, who died in 1740. Beneath the central inscribed slab lie the skull and crossbones and the motto 'memento mori'. The adjoining graveyard includes the graves of number of seamen.

The most remarkable part of Doon Point, Rathlin Island

1 SEPTEMBER 1815

DOON POINT, RATHLIN ISLAND

Here Mark Kerr's own description amply suffices: 'The basaltic pillars at Ushant or on the hill just above are the most perfect next to those at the Causeway itself that I have seen. I believe the curvature in them is observable only at the point scratched underneath which is the very easternmost part of Rathlin Island. These pillars are on the south side of the point. The northern side and eastern end (which continues to run into the sea for about thirty yards beyond the view below) have no decided pillars to be seen. The rock hereabouts can be compared to nothing but black sponge hardened into rock.'

The remains of Kinban Castle which stands on a lime stone Promontory of the same name about 2 miles West of Ballycastle

25 JULY 1809

KINBANE CASTLE

Kinbane Castle lies only a couple of miles west of Ballycastle, and on one occasion at least Mark Kerr made the journey by boat, as he drew a view of the castle from the sea. The ruin has altered little since he visited it, and this 1809 view from the west exhibits essentially the same features as today. The castle occupied a fine defensive position on a limestone promontory, accessible only via a narrow path down the adjacent cliff face leading up to the gate visible on the far right. Fronting the line of approach was a tower, originally built of basalt stone except for the angle quoins, which were picked out in white limestone, as at Carrickfergus. It has an unremarkable history, merely being recorded as newly built by Colla MacDonnell, Sorley Boy's elder brother, in 1551, and still occupied in the eighteenth century.

Kinban Castle from within

Kinban Castle, Barony of Cary Co. Antrim Ireland

An undated Kerr sketch shows the tower from the castle courtyard with the ground floor doorway, first floor window and line of weepholes at battlement level, which carried water from the wall tops – again essentially as at present. To the left is an outshot for a bed niche at first floor level. This is recorded as having partially collapsed around 1820. The drawing also appears to indicate the window which perhaps existed on the east side of this outshot. Other drawings show the castle on its prominent limestone promontory projecting into the Straits of Moyle, and a small boat drawn up on the shore to the east, perhaps the only place where a boat could come in. Only a very small boat could anchor here, which is odd given the obvious relationship of all the other MacDonnell castles to the sea.

Kinban Castle

Kinban Head and Castle   7 SEPTEMBER 1815

49

The flying bridge at Carrick a Rede 60 feet across and 84 feet above the Sea

CARRICK-A-REDE

Irish salmon which have grown to adulthood in the Atlantic Ocean return to spawn in the river in which they were born. At Carrick-a-Rede, or the rock in the road, generations of fishermen have erected a net between the mainland and a nearby island to catch these fish as they nose their way along the Antrim coast in search of their birthplace. To transport their catch home, the fishermen conceived the idea of erecting a rope bridge across the chasm between the mainland and the island. In Mark Kerr's day, as now, this bridge was an unmissable spectacle for visitors to the Antrim coast. Today the crossing can be made in safety via a modern rope bridge with adequate hand rails, side bracings and planking. In Kerr's time the situation was quite different. Three ropes were thrown across the gulf and short spars placed across them, about three feet apart. Two rows of narrow boards were then laid in a frighteningly haphazard fashion across the spars to form a bridge, of sorts, with a rope guide rail on one side. Few visitors were brave enough to make the crossing, and even the fishermen never made the trip without good reason. The bridge swung in the most alarming fashion above the sea some eighty feet below, and the skills of a ballet dancer were required to negotiate it safely. As well as salmon, it is said that sheep were carried across the bridge to graze on the island.

A graphic account written at the time of Kerr's visit describes how the salmon, once sighted, were encircled by the net and then landed, their capture being aided by those on the slopes above who hurled stones into the water to try to prevent the fish escaping.

Carrick a Rede Bridge – Kinban Head and Sheep Island in N. Coast of Antrim   1 SEPTEMBER 1815

1 SEPTEMBER 1838

DUNSEVERICK CASTLE

Dunseverick Castle lies right beside the coast road from Ballycastle to the Giant's Causeway, and would most certainly have captured Mark Kerr's attention as he passed by. It occupies the southern tip of a basalt stack extending into the sea, access being via a break in the precipitous sides of the stack onto a natural ramp leading up to a hollow in the top. From here it is easy to reach the remainder of the promontory. Mark Kerr shows the view from the south, with the castle perched on its rocky platform. The site is an ancient one, being recorded as a stronghold of the kingdom of Dal Riada, which spanned the northern region of the Irish Sea, an earlier fortification being attacked twice by Vikings. The present small tower, probably comprising two stories and an attic, is similar to the one at Kinbane and also thought to date from the sixteenth century. The ground floor must have been dark and largely featureless. The first floor was vaulted, with at least three windows, a recess perhaps for a bed, and possibly a very small latrine chamber. It was a private residential tower, with other accommodation located in buildings whose foundations may be observed to the north. The recess in the south-east angle weakened the structure, and in 1978 the corner fell. In this sketch Mark Kerr shows the tower very ruined, although in another done on the same day he shows it as substantially complete to gable level: perhaps an attempt to imagine it when inhabited. A drawing done in 1811 shows essentially the same view as the first one but transformed, as in his fantasy drawings, to render it almost like a camel, complete with a horse on its back.

1 SEPTEMBER 1838

Dunseverick Castle

18 AUGUST 1811

53

The Giant's Causeway

GIANT'S CAUSEWAY

The Giant's Causeway first became known to the wider world in the late seventeenth century through descriptions published by the Royal Society of London. Interest in the geological phenomenon and the surrounding landscape spread beyond the scientific community during the ensuing century, helped by the popularity of François Vivarès's engravings of the Causeway, which were based on sketches by the Dublin artist Susanna Drury. By the end of the eighteenth century the Causeway was an established spectacle to which every visitor to the north of Ireland made their way. Tourism soon became a significant factor in the local economy supporting a community of guides, souvenir sellers and boatmen. Improvements in communications during the nineteenth century such as the construction of the Antrim Coast Road in the 1830s and the arrival of the railway in the 1850s greatly increased visitor numbers and heralded the age of mass tourism.

Early drawings of the Causeway showed the area littered with broken columns and loose stones, by the end of the eighteenth century these had been swept away by insatiable souvenir hunters. Not content with loose stones, the more ambitious removed whole columns from the Causeway. The traveller and writer Richard Pococke oversaw the removal of a number of stones, both for scientific research and to decorate the Duchess of Portland's grotto.

The Causeway was situated in the heart of MacDonnell territory and its significance to the Antrim family can be gauged from the fact that, along with the old MacDonnell stronghold of Dunluce Castle, it was excluded from the division of the estate that followed the death of the 6th Earl in 1791. At the time these sketches were made the Causeway was the joint property of Anne Catherine, Countess of Antrim and Mark Kerr's wife, Charlotte. The Antrim family considered themselves guardians of the Causeway, and Mark Kerr took an active role in protecting it from the ravages of tourists.

In 1825, on hearing reports that the crew of a Royal Navy ship had removed a number of columns from the Causeway, Vice-Admiral Mark Kerr wrote to the Admiralty to complain. He explained that he was not writing merely to defend private property but because '… this causeway is considered not only one of the greatest wonders in Great Britain but throughout all Europe and the preservation of it a matter of general consequence to the whole world'. Although he received an apology from the ship's captain, he found the Admiralty uninterested in issuing orders for the protection of the Causeway.

Niel McMullan for 30 years Guide at the Giant's Causeway by Letitia Louisa Kerr

MONDAY 30 AUGUST 1838

In their role as guardians of the Causeway the Antrim family appointed local caretakers. The incumbent at the time of the incident with the naval ship and for many years after was Neal McMullan, who lived near-by at Black Rock. The caretaker's job was not an easy one. McMullan claimed he was threatened with a boat hook by the naval party, and later caretakers had frequent confrontations with souvenir hunters and enterprising local guides keen to sell them pieces of the Causeway.

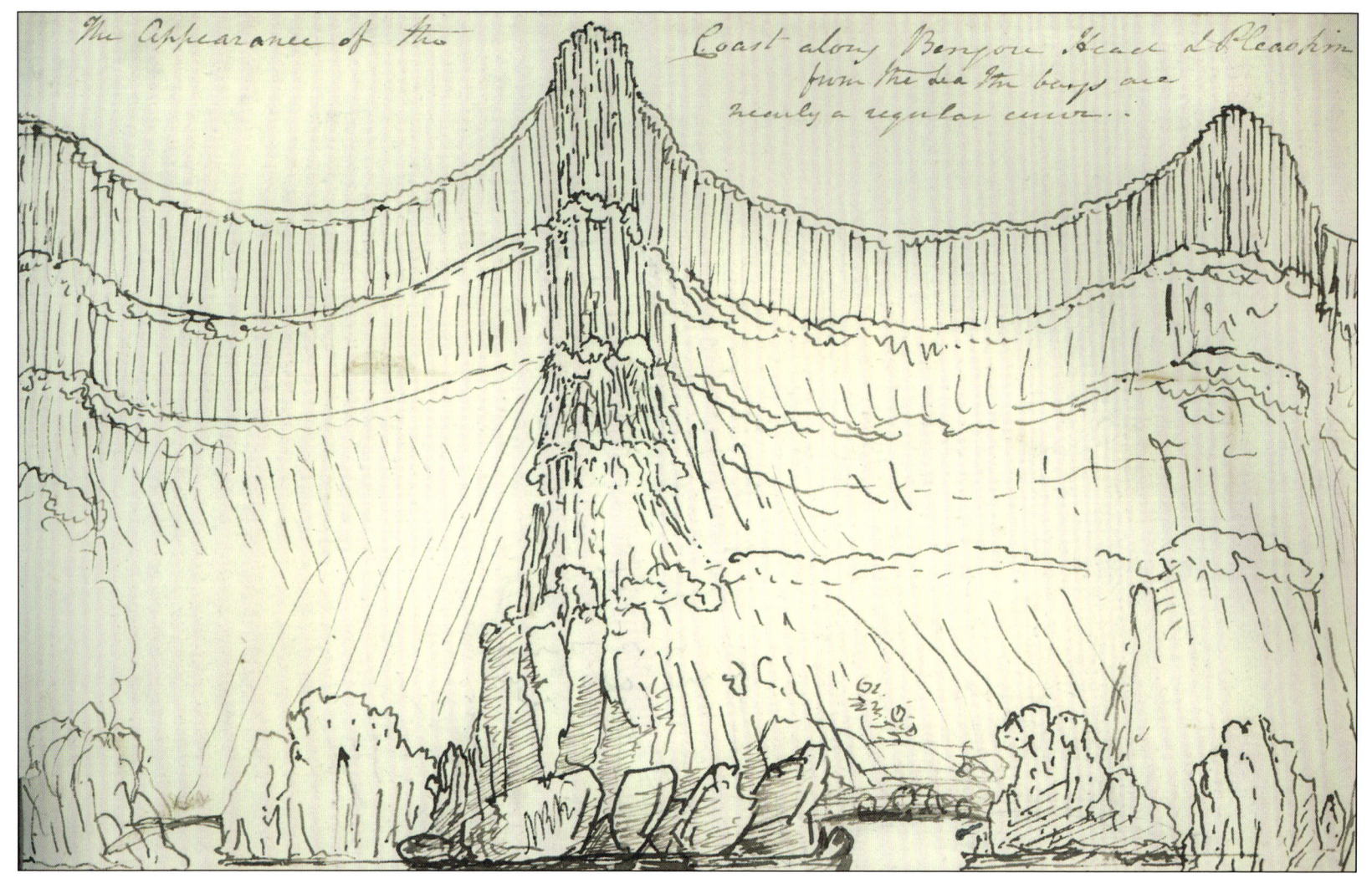

The Appearance of the Coast along Bengore Head and Pleaskin from the Sea.
The bays are nearly a regular curve.

The Antrim family's ownership of the Causeway was disputed by the Lecky family, who had acquired the surrounding land during the eighteenth century. Mark Kerr was drawn into an argument with Hugh Lecky in the 1830s when a pillar declaring the Causeway to be property of the Antrim estate was removed. The disagreement continued for the rest of the century, with the Lecky family going as far as to erect a house on the Causeway to reinforce their claims.

In 1896, the Leckys leased the Causeway to a consortium who erected fences and charged for admittance. This resulted in a famous court case in which Mark Kerr's grandson William, the 11th Earl of Antrim, lent his support to those campaigning for public access. The consortium won its case and the Causeway became a commercial attraction for many years. However, in 1961, the Northern Ireland region of the National Trust under the chairmanship of Mark Kerr's descendant Randal, 13th Earl of Antrim, acquired the property, and free public access was restored. In 1986, UNESCO designated the Causeway a World Heritage Site, endorsing Mark Kerr's view that '… the preservation of it is a matter of general consequence to the whole world'.

Pleaskin and the Coast near the Causeway

CAUSEWAY COAST

The striking impression that the coastline around Pleaskin Head made on Mark Kerr was amply supported by other visitors of the time. These included such veterans as the surveyors of the Ordnance Survey, who noted that although many who come to see scenery in the Causeway will no doubt be much disappointed, it is in the neighbouring coast that scenery of the most sublime and magnificent description is to be found, and that 'nothing can exceed the grandeur and exquisite beauty of the scenery in Port-na-Plaiskin and Port Reostan'. 'At Pleaskin Cape the columnar basalt is beautifully constructed in different strata in the upper part of the cliff, which is perpendicular to the horizon, representing alternate layers of rugged rocks and regular rows of pillars of 50 or 60 feet high, and at the bottom of the whole, a stratum of red ochre. From this the remainder of the cliff forms a rugged slope to the sea.'

Bengore Head

7 SEPTEMBER 1815

Ronan an Valle near the
Causeway Co Antrim
1833

Dunluce Castle from the Pound

DUNLUCE CASTLE

The ruins of Dunluce Castle lie on a rocky promontory close to the coast road between Portrush and Ballycastle, and they would have been a natural port of call for the Kerrs on their way to Portrush, which formed part of Charlotte's estates. The Kerrs paid for maintenance work to prevent any further deterioration to the ruins, so they were clearly very proud of this relic of the family's past. The MacDonnells had captured the stronghold of Dunluce from the MacQuillans in the 1550s, and afterwards substantially enlarged, strengthened and improved it. Their occupation continued until the mid-seventeenth century when the castle was largely dismantled by Cromwellian settlers. It was one of the strongest fortresses held by a native family anywhere in Ireland.

Mark Kerr drew the ruins of Dunluce Castle from all possible external angles, but there are no drawings whatsoever of its interior. This suggests he did not attempt to enter its precincts, which would have involved a hazardous expedition across the crumbling wall bridge, at the far left of this sketch, which spanned the gulf between the castle and the adjoining mainland.

The two prominent gables to the right of the drawing are the remains of the three-storey hall, where the Ist Earl of Antrim entertained his guests in a style befitting his prominence in early Stuart society. Although this was indeed an impressive building, with three sets of mullioned bay windows on its entrance front, it was surprisingly unostentatious in comparison with the houses of those of equivalent rank in England and, more especially, with those of the settler nobility in Ulster, such as Belfast Castle. The ground floor would have included a large hall and parlour, and above lay a great chamber for the family to dine with their guests, a withdrawing chamber and family or guest accommodation.

Dunluce Castle from
the East

AUGUST 1809

These two drawings were done before the collapse of the building on the northernmost edge of the rock, and clearly show its two gable ends still standing. A legend has developed that this range had fallen into the sea in the late 1630s, and that this caused the 2nd Earl of Antrim's wife, whose apartments it perhaps contained, to refuse to live in the castle any longer. The Kerr drawings show that at most only part of the seaward-facing façade could have collapsed into the sea at this time.

Dunluce Castle from the West

AUGUST 1809

These drawings show the half towers corbelled out at angles which were added to the gatehouse in the early seventeenth century. They were probably the work of Scottish masons, in whose native land they were known as 'studies'.

Entrance into Dunluce Castle
1838

Dunluce Castle Entrance side
1836

BALLYMAGARRY

Ballymagarry means the 'garden townland', and this fertile spot about a mile from Dunluce Castle may have been used to grow produce for consumption there, as well as serving as a deer park.

After the 2nd Earl of Antrim was restored to his estates by Charles II in 1663, he found that his former residence at Dunluce had been so badly despoiled by Cromwellian settlers that he decided to build a new mansion for himself at Ballymagarry. The Antrims used this house as the chief seat on their estates until it was destroyed by fire in 1750. After that its old park, pleasure grounds and gardens were abandoned in favour of Glenarm. An agent for the Antrim estates called Adam Hunter subsequently lived there, and built a house on the site of the old building.

An account written in 1838 describes Ballymagarry much as Mark Kerr must have seen it. 'Of the former splendid and extensive building nothing now remains to denote its existence at any period but about thirty-two feet in length, varying from twenty to thirty feet in height, of one end of a square, and on which the late Adam Hunter Esquire had a bell erected while residing at Ballymagarry House. This wall is of whin quarry stone and about two feet thick.'

Kerr's drawing therefore shows a portion of the only wall of the original Ballymagarry House that was still standing at the time of his visit, along with the bell added by the late family agent. As it is the only depiction of any part of the old house that now exists, and as even this fragment of a wall has long since vanished, this drawing is peculiarly tantalising.

Ballymagarry   18 AUGUST 1811

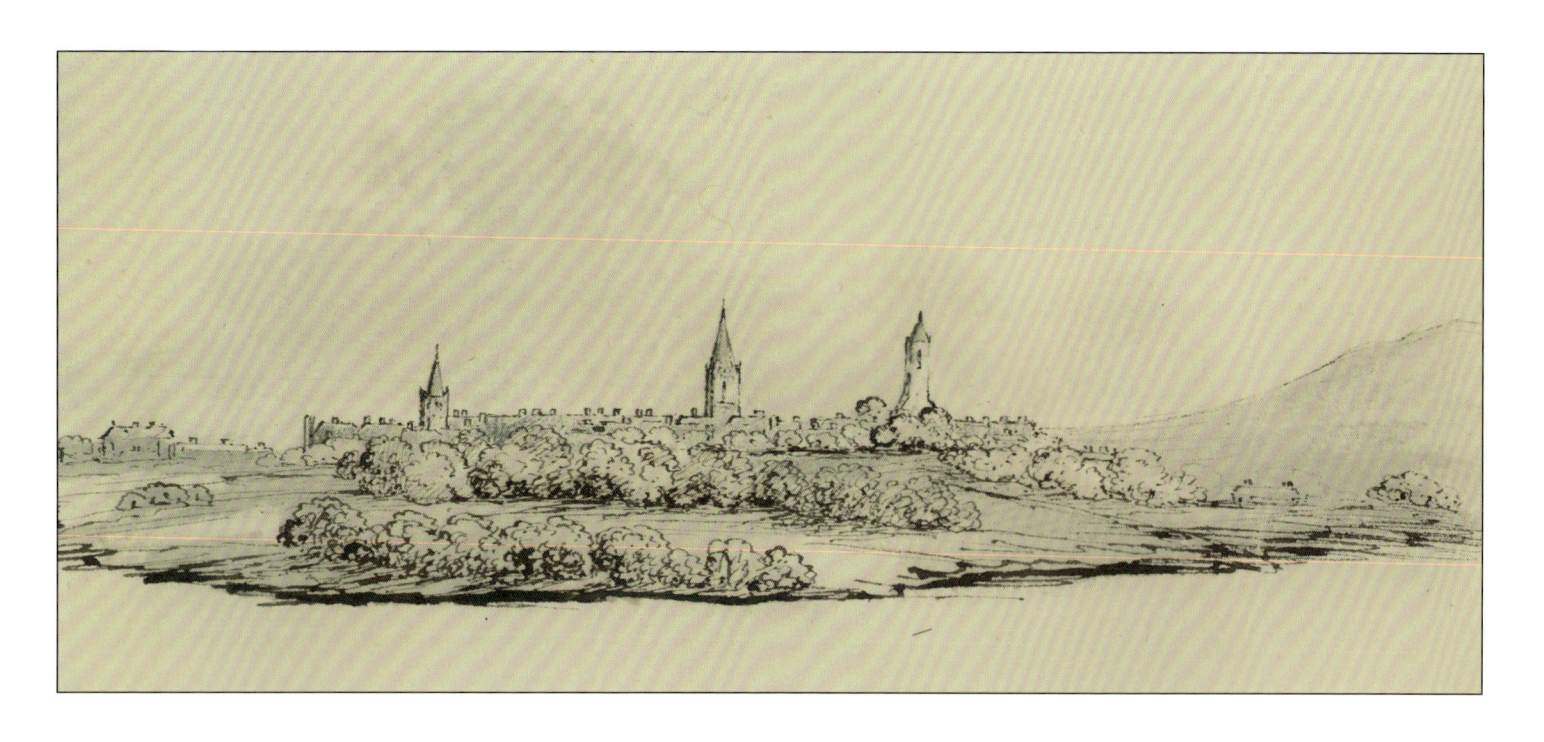

BALLYMONEY

Ballymoney was the largest town on Lady Charlotte's estate. In 1826, one of its principal streets, Pyper Row, was renamed Charlotte Street in her honour. The town held many memories for the couple, some sad and some happy. In 1834 their second son, Charles Fortescue, 'a noble creature', according to his father, died as a result of a chill contracted following a visit to Ballymoney to celebrate his becoming heir to his mother's estate. On 22nd October of the following year, Mark Kerr and his son Hugh Seymour set out once more for Ballymoney to attend a dinner in the King's Arms Hotel organised to welcome Hugh Seymour as the new Lord Dunluce following the death of his elder brother. Eighty-six gentlemen attended the function, who, following a splendid, bibulous meal, 'sat up till a late hour, and parted with reluctance'. Mark and Seymour spent the night as guests of the Leslie family at Leslie Hill, from whence they returned home, arriving, it is understood, just in time to witness Charlotte's death on the 26th.

Kerr's sketch shows the three spires which at the time contributed to give Ballymoney 'a pleasing and lively appearance': namely from left to right, the market house at the town end of Charlotte Street; the present parish church, built in 1783; and its seventeenth-century forerunner on the opposite side of the road – by the 1830s a ruin apart from its spire. An octagonal spire was added to the tower of the parish church in 1868, and a campanile to that of the market house in 1852, thus much altering their appearances from those depicted by Kerr. In his time the market house, erected about 1775 and now the Masonic Hall, was divided into three. The upper part comprised a gallery extending around the north, east and south walls, and two jury rooms, one on the east and another on the west. The central part was a court house, with a barristers' room leading off it; and the ground floor was used as a wet-weather market for agricultural produce. The building was also used a place of public worship and assembly. Attached to the west end was the former gaol. Although no prisoners were held here, a keeper was still paid an annual sum to care for it. The fine building on the left side of the drawing is presumably Leslie Hill.

Portrait of Mark Kerr drawn by Letitia Louisa Kerr for her mother   1824

    The former Northern Bank manager's house in High Street was originally assembly rooms built about 1760 by Charlotte's grandfather, the 5th Earl of Antrim – who had a passion for horse racing, to provide a venue for balls and other entertainments associated with the race meetings at Leaney, just south of the town. The building was subsequently leased by Mark Kerr to James Cramsie, with the stipulation that the ballroom be vacated at his behest to provide a venue for public entertainments.

    In 1835 Lady Charlotte and her husband graciously acceded to a petition by the townsfolk of Ballymoney against the renewal of tolls on marketable goods, which they greatly feared would affect the prosperity of the town. Mark Kerr also gave the land for a new Catholic chapel, consecrated in 1834, which replaced a primitive building known as 'the potato pit'; and waived the rent formerly paid by only one of the congregations within the town, namely that of the meeting house in the former malt kiln at Rodeing Foot.

Beardiville E.A. McNaghten Esq. Co Antrim   17 OCTOBER 1828

BEARDIVILLE

Kerr probably was either invited to or became interested in Beardiville House, near Portrush, during one of his family's visits to north Antrim, most likely that of 1826, but did not get around to making a finished drawing of it until 1828. This may explain certain inaccuracies such as his depiction of the windows as three panes wide when in fact they were only narrow, two-paned ones, and his over-emphasis of the doorcase. Kerr, nonetheless, accurately represents the armorial plaque above the front door, dated 1713, and there are other features, such as the narrow windows and heavy chimney-stacks, to suggest that the original house dates from around 1709, when the Macnaghten family took a lease of the property from the 4th Earl of Antrim. Mark Kerr's drawing also shows the attractive dormer windows, which were subsequently slated over, and lacks the single-storey wing added to the west sometime in the nineteenth century. An account written in 1835 described the house as 'good and commodious but old fashioned'.

In Kerr's day, Beardiville was the home of Edmond A. Macnaghten, the elder son of Edmund 'Beardy' Macnaghten, so-called either because he reputedly never cut his nails or hair, or simply because he was the proprietor of Beardiville. Edmund was the friend and agent of the 5th Earl of Antrim, and his portrait, complete with flowing beard, hangs today in Glenarm Castle. He was another sharp operator, skillfully enriching himself by purchasing choice portions of the Antrim estate on favourable terms, and sending the proceeds, however modest, to an Earl delighted to receive contributions to support his spendthrift ways. In the election of 1806 Mark Kerr had supported Edmond A. Macnaghten's candidacy for the Antrim parliamentary seat, whilst his brother-in-law Sir Harry Vane-Tempest supported a rival candidate. Macnaghten entered into the dispute with such gusto that he even threatened Sir Harry with a duel.

Portrush

9 SEPTEMBER 1815

PORTRUSH

Portrush was the second most important town on Lady Charlotte's estate. Mark Kerr obviously took a keen interest in its well-being as he built the bath house in 1834 and gave the site for the Church of Ireland church. Mark Street and Kerr Street are named after him. This sketch commemorates a boat trip he made to the town in 1815 and shows the former landing place before the present harbour was built. Portrush or Portrosse, which means 'the port of the promontory', had been a landing place for many centuries, and this sketch also shows the hill adjacent to the harbour, the inner face of which was substantially quarried away to construct the present harbour.

Not only was the village home to local fishermen, but French fishing boats were known to call in from time to time. In addition, the landing place served as the main winter port for cargo for Coleraine, as ships could not enter the river Bann in bad weather. Larger ships would shelter from storms off the Skerries, north-east of Portrush, from whence their cargo was brought ashore in smaller boats.

Port Rush from the Sea

29 OCTOBER 1833

This sketch shows the north pier or quay with the fishing fleet of smacks pulled up on to the pier. In 1826 the merchants of Coleraine came together to form the Portrush Harbour Company, and employed the engineer John Rennie to design and construct a new harbour. The project took a number of years to complete, the north pier being built first. The rock fill required for its construction came from the hill behind the harbour. In 1829 the amount of rock deposited in the making of the north and south piers was over 100,000 tons, and by 1830 this amounted to over 250,000 tons. Further extensions to the piers were added over the years, and a new pier was proposed on the north-east side of Ramore Head in 1859.

At low tide the depth of water in the new harbour was twenty-seven feet, and it could thus accommodate ships and steamboats of a large size. These came from as far afield as Derry, Liverpool and Glasgow, as shipping still could not get into the mouth of the River Bann in the winter or in storms. As a consequence, Portrush became a port of considerable significance, and grew in size and prosperity accordingly.

A substantial parliamentary grant was obtained in 1864 for the construction of moles or embankments at the mouth of the river Bann to counteract silting and increase accessibility. Work does not appear to have been completed until 1882, resulting in a loss of traffic to Portrush.

Port Rush   SEPTEMBER 1833

CLOGH CASTLE, COUNTY ANTRIM

Mark Kerr had a special reason to visit Clogh on his way to stay at Antrim Castle in 1815 as Randal Arranagh, the 1st Earl of Antrim, built a castle to serve the manor he established here. The castle is believed to have comprised two sections, with a ditch between them, encircled by an outer ditch and curtain wall. There were buildings in the southern section, but the ruined gatehouse depicted by Kerr lay in the northerly part. Fragments of the gatehouse still survive but the southern section of the castle was quarried away in the 1920s and 30s. Large pieces of fallen masonry make examination of the gatehouse difficult today, but it is clear that it was a distinctly irregular building, with neither gateway being centred in its respective wall.

The remains of the Old Castle at Clogh

9 OCTOBER 1815

Mount at Antrim Castle 23 AUGUST 1828

ANTRIM MOTTE

This motte was the most prominent part of the castle of Antrim, which acted as the administrative centre of the County of Antrim, one of five counties or bailiwicks of the Earldom of Ulster, which encompassed most of counties Antrim and Down. Records show that this castle was in existence by 1211, and it was garrisoned during a war which took place that year. Money was spent at this time on buildings in the castle and a barn and byre, presumably located in a courtyard attached to the motte. The castle was also the hub of a farm large enough to justify six plough teams of oxen. It continued to be the administrative centre of the county until the mid-fourteenth century, when a town is recorded at Antrim. Enough apparently survived for it still to be regarded as the focal point of the county in the early seventeenth century, when Sir Hugh Clotworthy built a new house on the site.

The motte subsequently became an integral part of the formal gardens that were created around Antrim Castle in the late seventeenth and early eighteenth centuries, elements of which survive to this day, and by far the best view of the gardens could be obtained from its summit. At about the time of the Kerr drawing a yew hedge was planted flanking the spiral path to the summit of the motte, which was crowned with Scots Pine. The beautifully kept grounds surrounding the castle were open to the public at all times, and were an extremely popular destination for both local residents and visitors.

Antrim Castle											14 SEPTEMBER 1811

ANTRIM CASTLE

The Massereene family of Antrim Castle were distant connections of Lady Charlotte's. The original house had been erected in stages between 1610 and 1662 by the important English settler Sir Hugh Clotworthy, and his son, Sir John Clotworthy, who was created 1st Viscount Massereene in 1660. It was three storeys high and quadrangular in shape, each corner being marked by a square tower, and was chiefly noted for its highly decorated doorway, including the head of Charles 1. A quirky feature was a platform on the roof, accessed by a ladder from within, which could be used for dining *alfresco* by employing a pulley to hoist up the necessary furniture and provisions.

By the late 1700s the family's finances were in a precarious position, and the castle was 'hastening rapidly to decay'. Disaster was kept at bay by the marriage of Harriet Skeffington, who became Viscountess Massereene in her own right, to the son of John Foster, the last Speaker of the Irish House of Commons.

The Kerrs are first thought to have visited the castle in 1811, the year after Harriet's nuptials, and Mark Kerr sketched the front of the house, in danger, it appears, of being subsumed by the vegetation fringing the adjacent riverbank. The castle cannot have been derelict, however, as the Kerrs were accommodated there. The frontage of the building depicted by Mark Kerr has much in common with the principal front of the house which resulted from building work completed in 1813, showing clearly that this work comprised merely the remodelling and embellishment of an existing building, not its reconstruction, as sometimes stated. The castle was burnt in 1922, and almost entirely demolished in 1970.

Cedar Antrim Castle   23 AUGUST 1828

ANTRIM CASTLE GATEHOUSE

The crenellated castle-style gatehouse is understood to have been built in 1818. Mark Kerr, when visiting Antrim Castle in 1828, would have undoubtedly been keen to sketch such a romantic and picturesque new feature of the park. The gatehouse provided a splendid approach to the castle from the market place in the town, and included accommodation for the warder who operated the machinery for opening the heavy oak gates. On the north side of the drive from the gatehouse to the castle lay a terraced garden full of beautiful flowers, raised some nine feet off the ground, which had been formed out of the seventeenth-century bastions commanding the town.

Mark Kerr had a passion for ancient and venerable trees: the more gnarled and misshapen they were the better he liked them. This fine cedar was probably a relic of the late-seventeenth- and early-eighteenth-century plantings, and would have been far too enticing a subject to pass by.

Cedar at Antrim Castle
13 AUGUST 1815

73

ANTRIM ROUND TOWER

One of the highlights of Mark Kerr's visit to Antrim Castle in October 1815 was an expedition to the most famous local landmark, the c. tenth-century round tower known as 'the Steeple', which lay on the outskirts of Antrim town, and was formerly part of an Early Christian monastic settlement. The height he gives for the tower on his sketch corresponds reasonably with the 1838 Ordnance Survey figure of ninety-two feet. The survey also notes that most of the upper six feet of the cone, which was twelve feet high, had been knocked off, apparently by lightening, at 'some remote period', but repaired in 1819. Presumably the Ordnance Survey was misinformed as to the date of the damage, for Mark Kerr's 1815 drawing shows the tower and cone substantially intact, supporting Dubourdieu's 1812 observation in his statistical account of County Antrim that 'the tower at Antrim is in a much higher state of preservation than any of the others; it tapers curiously towards the top, and its roof (of flat stones) is very good'.

Significantly Mark Kerr draws the same large rough stones being used densely packed together all the way up to the top of the tower, whereas much of the stonework at the level of the top storey now comprises smaller stones and larger quantities of mortar than would have been used in the original construction. His drawing also suggests that the earlier cap was constructed of much finer stonework than the present one.

Kerr shows one of the four windows in the top of the tower, which faced, more or less, north, east, south or west, and the doorway, which was then seven feet above the ground. Virtually all round towers have elevated doorways. This was most probably a security or defensive measure, though it was not foolproof. Customarily these doorways faced the west entrance of the monastery church, and access was presumably by wooden stairs or ladders, which in this case have disappeared, as have the several internal wooden floors.

At Antrim 97 feet high, 16 feet diameter   10 OCTOBER 1815

Shane's Castle from Byfield Cottage

22 AUGUST 1828

Kerr was clearly excited by this enigmatic building. At the time there were many different theories circulating about the age and origin of these strange towers. It was generally accepted that they dated from the Early Christian period, but whereas some were of the opinion that the elevated doorways were a form of defence against Viking attacks, others thought the towers had been constructed by these invaders, who had brought many artistic and technical advances into Early Christian Ireland. A minority held the view that the towers were remnants of an ancient pagan civilisation.

They were indeed of native construction, but are always found at monastic sites, and the earliest examples can be dated to the tenth century. The original Irish name for them, *clog tigh*, translates as bell houses, and reveals their basic function, which was to act as bell towers to broadcast the religious hours to their monastic communities. They were by far the tallest buildings of their time in Ireland, and were highly prestigious constructions.

BIRCH HILL, ANTRIM

Whilst guests of the Massereene family at Antrim Castle in October 1815, Mark Kerr also made an excursion to nearby Birch Hill, about a mile north-east of Antrim town, which seems at the time to have been the property of Miss Bristow, whose family had been agents to the Massereenes in the latter part of the eighteenth century. The house was famed not for its architecture, but more for it's tastefully laid out grounds and gardens, complete with a valuable collection of plants. Most spectacular of all was the prospect it enjoyed. It lay on rising ground above Lough Neagh, and on clear days offered the visitor stupendous views over the nearby round tower, Antrim deer park and the parkland and plantings of Shane's Castle, and glimpses of counties Derry, Tyrone and Armagh on the farther shores.

Birch Hill   10 OCTOBER 1815

Nonetheless, Mark Kerr's drawing of the house is significant, as there appears to be no other view of Birch Hill in the years following its completion around 1785. His drawing reflects an 1838 description, which records that it was 'not modern in its appearance but is in good order and is a comfortable and gentleman-like family residence. It is two-storey and spacious'. It was subsequently renamed Ardnaveigh, and was destroyed by fire in 1941. The outbuildings and offices, including the walled garden, remain in the grounds of St Malachy's High School.

Birch Hill and Cottage   16 SEPTEMBER 1811

BYFIELD COTTAGE, ANTRIM

Byfield Cottage, the pretty home of Miss McCleverty, the major tenant of Birch Hill townland in 1833, probably lay within easy walking distance to the south-east of Birch Hill house, and enjoyed the same magnificent views over Lough Neagh. Miss McCleverty is presumably the elderly lady who in retirement lived near Larne Lough in a venerable house beside the ruined church at Glynn, said to have been linked to the church by an underground passage. She obviously had a liking for quirky abodes as she also owned another ornamental cottage, this time handsomely situated beside the waterfall at Glenoe, inland from Glynn, a place much frequented by picknickers from the neighbouring towns.

Byfield Cottage was demolished sometime around the middle of the nineteenth century, and no images of it are thought to exist apart from those done by Mark Kerr. Miss McCleverty's cottage, as depicted by him, was an extremely picturesque, thatched, L-shaped dwelling, with delightful oval or round-headed windows. It had much in common with Raymond Cottage, situated in Drumraymond townland on the south-eastern shore of Lough Beg, which was constructed for Henrietta Frances O'Neill, wife of the Hon. John O'Neill of Shane's Castle, in about 1777. This cottage was made from wooden frames pre-fabricated at Shane's Castle, and then re-erected in its intended location. Byfield Cottage may, quite possibly, have been another product of the Shane's Castle workshop.

It is easy to imagine the Massereenes, anxious to occupy their guests in the long interval between mid-morning breakfast and early evening dinner, encouraging them to drive out to Birch Hill, stroll around the gardens and wonder at the view, before enjoying tea on the lawn with the Misses Bristow or McCleverty.

Byfield 12 OCTOBER 1815

Bifield Cottage Miss McCleverty APRIL 1826

77

Ram Island North

18 SEPTEMBER 1838

RAM'S ISLAND, LOUGH NEAGH

This tadpole-shaped island, off the east coast of Lough Neagh, was acquired by the first and only Earl O'Neill sometime shortly after 1810. He laid it out in the most tasteful manner, complete with plantations, beautifully laid turf and many walks. On the fatter, southern end he built a neat thatched cottage, which he filled with costly rustic furniture. The O'Neill coat of arms occupied a prominent position on the main front. This cottage was vandalized during the Second World War and is now a ruin. Mark Kerr shows the terrace immediately in front of the cottage, which sloped down to the lough. Since the time of the Kerr drawing the level of the lough has been substantially lowered, and the terrace no longer abuts the shore. There was also a six-sided cottage for a caretaker. Close beside lay the remains of an ancient round tower, three-storeys high with an elevated doorway.

Mark Kerr also includes the flagstaff which the contemporary Ordnance Survey map shows to have been located on the south-western side of the island. An accompanying Ordnance Survey memoir described Ram's Island as 'one of the most picturesque spots on Lough Neagh'. Mark Kerr obviously concurred with this assessment, as did the 'parties of pleasure from all the counties round the lough', who came to picnic there.

Olderfleet Castle Co Antrim   EASTER 1826

OLDERFLEET CASTLE, LARNE

Oldefleet Castle lies on a promontory known as Curran Point, which juts into Larne Lough to the south of Larne Harbour. Larne Lough was once known as Olderfleet, and this castle was one of three guarding its entrance. Kerr depicts the view of the castle from the north, showing the interior of the south wall of what is probably a sixteenth-century tower house. Tower houses are the prevalent monument from the secular life of fifteenth- and sixteenth-century Ireland, and their purpose was to provide a secure and comfortable residence for a gentry family and its servants. Within Ulster, they are most often encountered in south-east County Down, reflecting the survival of an Anglo-Irish gentry in this area after the collapse of the Earldom of Ulster in the fourteenth century.

Olderfleet Castle has double-splayed windows at ground level, probably to let in more light, but they would also have given more traverse for hand-guns. The distribution of structures possessing this feature has a strong County Down bias. In Mark Kerr's drawing, the ground floor at Olderfleet is obscured by a low building whose south wall still exists, partially overlapping the ruined north wall of the tower, and now appearing at first sight like a bawn wall.

All the three openings in the tower depicted by Kerr have been recently restored with new stonework, but with the first floor window arch more segmental in shape than the nearly semi-circular arch shown on the drawing, and the two upper ones equally segmental and not nearly square as shown in the drawing.

Carrickfergus Castle

EASTER 1826

CARRICKFERGUS CASTLE

Carrickfergus Castle, strategically located on a rocky promontory of Belfast Lough, was the chief castle of the Norman Earldom of Ulster, which from 1177 was ruled over by John de Courcy. He was a prolific builder, founding Inch and Black Abbeys, and beginning Dundrum Castle as well as St Nicholas's Church at Carrickfergus, and the massive keep and the inner ward of its castle. The keep, at the top of Kerr's drawing, consisted of three storeys above a basement, and was entered at first floor level. It provided impressive domestic accommodation. The other buildings of the inner ward, including the great hall, do not survive.

De Courcy was ejected by Hugh de Lacy in 1204, and the castle was wrested from him by King John in 1210, under whose constable, de Serlane, a new curtain wall was constructed in 1217, creating a middle ward. This wall only survives at its two ends, at the west and along the eastern, seaward side, the rest having been razed to the ground c. 1700. In 1227, three years after unsuccessfully attempting to regain Carrickfergus by force, de Lacy had the castle restored to him by Henry III, and he remained in possession at his death in 1242. It was probably during this period that the final curtain wall was thrown up and the outer ward and gatehouse built. The gatehouse originally consisted of two fully circular towers with a wooden entrance; the present vaulted passage dates from the earlier fourteenth century.

The collapse of the Earldom of Ulster in 1333 left Carrickfergus isolated from other English-controlled areas of Ireland, and it was not until the subjugation of the north of the country in the late sixteenth century that it regained its importance. Alterations were made in the 1560s, including the reconstruction of the gatehouse towers, insertion of lower stores in a large medieval building to the east of the outer ward, and provision of brick-built embrasures for cannon, internal dividing walls and a great arch over the third floor within the keep. In 1688–9 the castle was held for James II, and in 1760 it was temporarily captured by the French, but otherwise it remained under Crown control. It was adapted as an infantry barrack c. 1800 when the gate towers were lowered, a fourth floor inserted into the keep and barracks built on either side of the outer ward, of which the officers' quarters partly survive.

This 1826 view of the castle from the north-east was probably done by Mark Kerr on his way to catch the paddle steamer service which had just been introduced at Donaghadee, and shows that there has been little change to this outstanding landmark since his time. His drawing does, however, include the aperture at the top right of the keep, which was opened up when the castle was converted into a store and barrack during the Napoleonic Wars. This opening was subsequently blocked up. In Kerr's time there were also chimneys on what was then the Officers' Mess along the north-east curtain wall. These, too, have since been removed. In contrast, the setting of the castle has suffered a dramatic change since Kerr made his visit, due to the construction of the Marine Highway between the castle and the town in the 1960s.

Coast between Tor Point and Cushendun   1833

Belvoir Co of Downe, Ireland. Seat of Arthur Hill Trevor. Viscount Dungannon

View of Belvoir the residence of Viscount Dungannon taken in 1805

BELVOIR PARK, NEWTOWNBREDA

Belvoir Park was the Irish seat of Arthur Hill-Trevor, 5th Viscount Dungannon, Lady Charlotte's half-brother, former guardian, and one of the executors of her father's will, who, in addition, owned a large estate at Brynkinalt in Wales. He was also acquainted with the Kerrs, having toured Europe with Mark Kerr's eldest brother, Lord Ancram, in the 1780s.

In 1802, the acrimonious dispute over the disposition of the Antrim family estates necessitated a visit by the Kerrs to Ireland. Relations between Charlotte and her elder sister, Anne Catherine, were, to put it bluntly, atrocious, and the possibility of staying at Glenarm therefore unthinkable. Lord Dungannon came to the rescue and offered the Kerrs accommodation at Belvoir Park. He had not resided at Belvoir since the mid-1790s, and, as a result, it had been substantially neglected.

Belvoir formerly Lord Dungannon's residence in the County of Downe

The house itself was still habitable, and was the home of his agent, Captain Cortland Skinner, and his young family. For Lady Charlotte, the opportunity to stay at Belvoir brought reminders of childhood visits with her family, and the intrigue and excitement of the masquerade balls of her youth.

Either during this stay, or another in 1805, Mark Kerr appears to have made two drawings of the house, one of the entrance front and the other of the east front, which almost certainly became the models for watercolours. Belvoir Park, as depicted by him, was a three-storey affair, with a fine Ionic portico on the north front, affording guests in the dining room behind it splendid views of Cave Hill.

Belvoir formerly Lord Dungannon's residence in the County of Downe

    The addition of the third storey has been generally understood to have taken place about 1820, after the estate had become the property of the Bateson family, but the Kerr sketches reveal that it must have been completed well before this, almost certainly in the late 1780s. No trace of the house remains today.

    Mark Kerr's drawings include the spire of Knockbreda parish church, completed in 1737 to a design by the renowned architect Richard Castle. The church was built for Anne, Dowager Viscountess Midleton on land made available to her by her son, who was to become the 4th Viscount Dungannon.

An unfinished sketch of Hillsborough

1833

HILLSBOROUGH

Mark Kerr settled himself in a spot south of Hillsborough to sketch the fort perched on its mount and lake to the east. To the north lies St Malachi's Church, built by Wills Hill, Earl of Hillsborough, and first used for worship in 1773, which has been described as 'the most sophisticated and uniform example of the Georgian style in Ireland'. It is an unusually grand church for eighteenth-century Ireland, and Lord Hillsborough may have envisaged it becoming a cathedral church as Downpatrick Cathedral was then in ruins. Mark Kerr shows the fine spire and towers at the end of the transepts. His effort is described as an unfinished sketch, and its many distortions and misrepresentations indicate that it was done from a very inadequate recollection of the true situation on the ground. For instance, the square transept towers of the church and spear-shaped corner bastions of the fort itself are not accurately depicted, and 'the castle' on the north-west front, which forms the main entrance to the fort, is distinctly over-emphasised.

Hillsborough Fort, the earliest real artillery fortification in County Down, was probably completed in the 1650s, to command 'the chiefest roade' from Dublin to Carrickfergus. In the mid-eighteenth century the former gatehouse was heightened and battlemented, pointed doors and windows inserted, and square, battlemented corner towers added, thereby transforming it into a picturesque toy fort in the fashionable Gothic style, which became known as 'the castle'. At around the same time new vehicle entrances were broken through, opposite to each other, at the centre of the north-east and south-west sides of the fort, and a delightful Gothic gazebo built over the north-east entrance, along with the small round turrets, or sentry boxes, on the east and west bastions. Flower gardens were created on top of the all the bastions, and fine views over the adjacent church and lake were to be had from the ramparts. In Mark Kerr's day the fort appears to have been used as a pleasure ground for the Hill family, and in the year his drawing was made it was the setting for a great *alfresco* feast.

Mount Stewart and the Morne Mountains in the distance   8 AUGUST 1815

MOUNT STEWART, COUNTY DOWN

Mark Kerr visited Mount Stewart, the home of Robert Stewart, Earl and subsequently 1st Marquess of Londonderry, on several occasions, and sketched the house and its surroundings. He was well-acquainted with Lord Londonderry's elder son, Lord Castlereagh, since Lady Castlereagh's half-sister was married to his eldest brother, Lord Ancram. By the time of the Kerrs' visits Lord and Lady Londonderry were elderly, but their children were Mark Kerr's contemporaries.

The Londonderrys' public profile and status in society had risen meteorically due to Castlereagh's successful political career, and Mount Stewart became quite inadequate for the kind of hospitality now expected of them. In the first years of the nineteenth century it was transformed by the addition of a splendidly decorated new west wing, comprising a suite of interconnected rooms for entertaining, designed by the celebrated London architect, George Dance. The intention was to rebuild the remainder of the house at a future date. Kerr's drawings of Mount Stewart are the only ones known showing the interim stage between the Dance addition and the later alterations. They reveal that the spanking new wing was tacked onto a delightfully rambling, higgledy-piggledy mass of buildings to the east. The house was entered through Dance's coach porch on the north front, which was 'extremely convenient at night and bad weather to drive under'.

Mount Stewart House

11 AUGUST 1811

Mt Stewart

16 OCTOBER 1815

Mount Stewart 15 NOVEMBER 1809

To show off his home to best effect, Robert Stewart transformed its surroundings into a fine park in the fashionable style, circumnavigated by a perimeter drive, and enlivened by a series of picturesque Gothic buildings. By 1809 this work was substantially complete, and Mark Kerr's visit that year may have been prompted by his desire to inspect and illustrate these improvements, which included a pair of new lodges at the western approach, and a fine lawn around the house, 'one of the most beautiful and extensive in this province'. Its construction was made possible by a realignment of the Portaferry road, so that it no longer passed right beside the south side of the house.

A striking revelation of Mark Kerr's sketches is the role played by the Temple of the Winds as a focal point and eye-catcher to the east. The subsequent growth of surrounding trees considerably lessened its impact in the landscape.

The financial records of the estate show that work commenced in 1793 on the construction of an embankment along the lough shore beside the house, the initial phase being completed by 1803, when heightening and repairs were undertaken. Confusingly, the Kerr sketches seem to show this area covered in water.

Temple at Mount Stewart

17 SEPTEMBER 1811

A bit of Mount Stewart 1815

A Cromlech or ancient place of interment at Mount Stewart. On removing many 1000 Cartloads of stones this was found underneath and inside it were two earthen Pots or Jars containing ashes. It is about 9 feet long and 4 broad.

21 OCTOBER 1815

CROMLECH AT MOUNT STEWART

Much confusion and misunderstanding surrounds the history of this monument. It is referred to by Kerr as a cromlech or type of prehistoric stone burial chamber generally covered with earth, but was in fact another type of burial known as a multiple-cist cairn. It was located in the Temple Meadow, north-east of the Temple of the Winds.

From the mid-eighteenth century onwards, agricultural improvements became a major preoccupation of landowners, an enthusiasm shared by Robert Stewart. Aided and abetted by his land stewards, he introduced new crops and better breeds of livestock to Mount Stewart, and improved the quality of the land by raising its fertility and installing proper drainage. This was before the mass-production of clay drainage pipes, and drain-making depended on a plentiful supply of stones. The pile of stones, perhaps some six to eight feet high and thirty feet in diameter, which made up the cairn covering this monument, proved too attractive a temptation, and around 1786 it was removed. Beneath the cairn were a large rectangular central cist, or stone burial chamber, and fifteen smaller ones. No finds are recorded from the central cist, but each smaller one contained a food vessel, accompanied by cremated bones and charcoal.

The central cist and one of the smaller ones were said to have been moved and reconstructed in a nearby location in the 1930s, when the 7th Marquess of Londonderry, perhaps still Secretary of State for Air, and a qualified pilot himself, found the Temple Meadow the perfect site for his own private airstrip. Sadly, all that remains of the multiple-cist cairn today are three rectangular slabs, probably capstones, and two smaller stones.

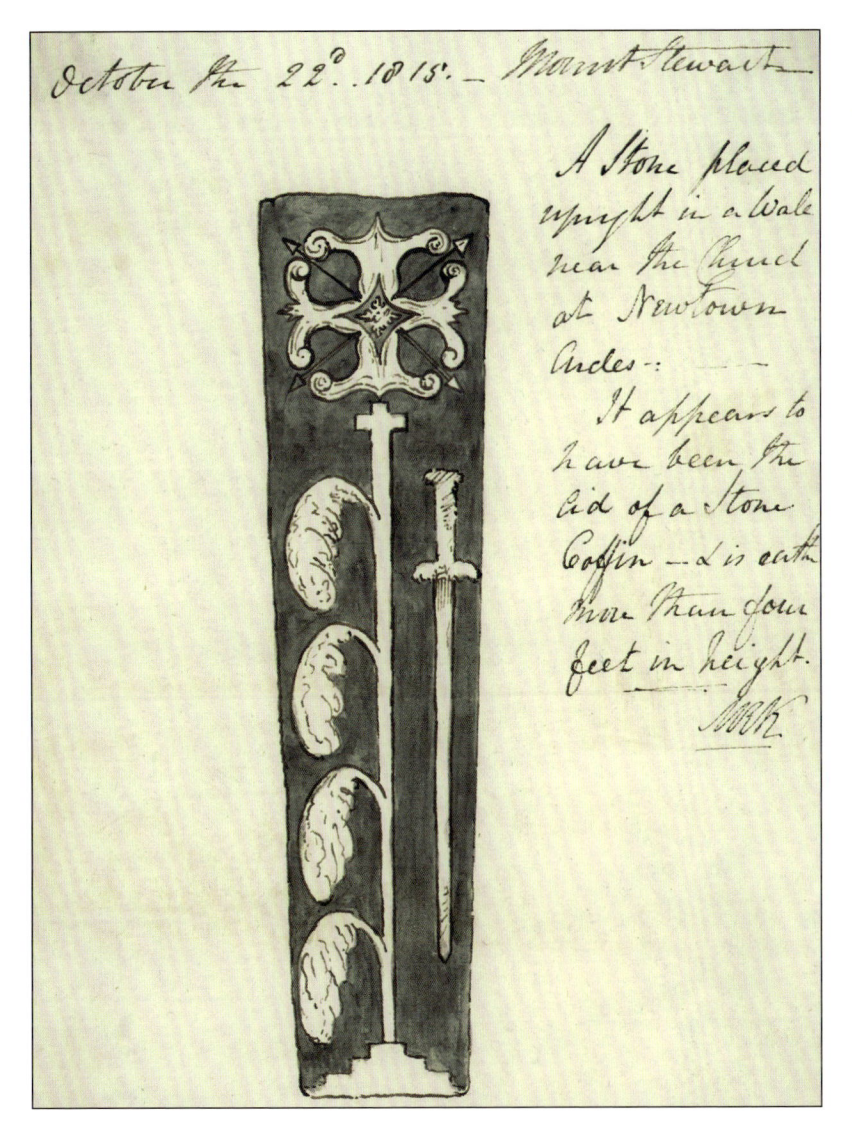

A Stone placed upright in a Wall near the Church at Newtown Ardes. It appears to have been the lid of a Stone Coffin and is easily more than four feet in height.

22 OCTOBER 1815

GRAVE SLAB AT NEWTOWNARDS

The day after drawing the cromlech at Mount Stewart Mark Kerr depicted another intriguing antiquity, namely a graveslab over four feet in height which had been inserted into a wall near the church in Newtownards. It is still to be seen today in St Mark's Church. The branch of stonemasonry which produced ornamental slabs to mark graves was one of the crafts introduced into the Earldom of Ulster during the thirteenth century. This craft is thought to have focused on the sandstone quarries on Scrabo Hill, at the northern end of Strangford Lough, which provided some of the best stone for carving in Ulster. The designs employed by the masons were based on those found in the north of England, from whence the carvers presumably originated. The slabs themselves are only found in eastern County Down and at Carrickfergus and Kilroot. They must have largely depended on boats sailing to Belfast and Carrickfergus for their distribution, which centred on the town of Newtownards. From thence these heavy, unwieldy items were transported short distances, but do not seem, for instance, to have reached as far as the English areas of south Antrim. The widespread movement of goods within the Earldom was dependent on pack-horses and carts, whose activities were hampered by a scarcity of roads with decent surfaces and moderate gradients.

93

Flax Windmill near Mount Stewart   4 NOVEMBER 1809

WINDMILLS NEAR MOUNT STEWART

It has not been possible to identify the precise location of either mill depicted by Mark Kerr, but they may have been mills associated specifically with the Mount Stewart estate. This is particularly likely in the case of the flax windmill with its unusual Gothic windows. These might indicate it to be a picturesque estate building, and Robert Stewart is known to have constructed a number of Gothic buildings within the park surrounding Mount Stewart in the early 1800s.

The flax windmill depicted by Mark Kerr has a stone tower with two Gothic windows, four common sails – where the canvas was spread on the sail frame, and a cap with a thatched conical roof and polygonal weather-boarded sides. There is also a 'tail' to the back of the cap, presumably to turn the sails to wind. A close examination of the cap and tail shows a doorway at the back of the cap and a ladder staircase leading down the tail. We are thus not dealing with a traditional windmill where the

A Windmill near Mt Stewart

NOVEMBER 1809

cap rotates about a fixed tower, but a post mill, where the cap and body are one and rotate about a central post supported within the basal tower. The tail would have been used to turn the buck – as the rotating part of the post mill is called, and the ladder to access it internally. Post mills were generally used for milling grain and are generally found in eastern England. Some are also recorded in Ireland, but generally in seventeenth century Plantation contexts.

It is difficult to imagine how scutching machinery could have been accommodated in the buck whilst allowing it to rotate. It is possible, but unlikely, that it was a hollow post mill – now only found in the Netherlands. Here, the rotative power of the sails was transmitted down through the buck into the tower below, where the machinery was housed.

How far the sketch should be viewed as an accurate record of the situation on the ground is debatable given that the shaft to which the sails are secured appears too far down the buck, and the sails look a bit short – they needed to come close to the ground in order to furl the canvas.

The second depiction of a windmill is slightly more plausible in that it has a tail-pole, tail-wheel and ladder. Also the buck is rectangular (the normal plan form), with a hipped roof and all weather-boarded. There would be no problem accommodating millstones in the buck. Again, there seem to be some inaccuracies, similar to those in sketch of the flax windmill. Moreover, the drawing shows the tailwheel affixed to the end of the ladder – in reality it would have been on the end of the actual tailpole.

Part of Grey Abbey near Mount Stewart   7 NOVEMBER 1809

GREY ABBEY, COUNTY DOWN

On his visits to Mount Stewart in 1809 and 1815, Mark Kerr seems to have spent a considerable amount of time drawing the nearby ruins of Geyabbey in great detail. The abbey was founded in the late twelfth century for the Cistercians of Holm Cultram by Affreca, wife of John de Courcy, who conquered Ulster in 1177 and founded nearby Inch Abbey in the early 1180s.

The church lies to the north of the complex, and was originally divided into two: the choir, transepts and crossing for the literate, superior choir monks, and the nave for the lay brothers, who were illiterate and did much of the hard manual labour of the community. The building along the east of the cloister was the chapter house, where the community met each day for business. Above lay the choir monks' dormitory, linked by a stair into the south transept so that they could go directly into the choir to participate in night offices. The south side of the cloister was occupied by the monks' refectory, while the lay brothers' dormitory and refectory was set along the west side. Right across Europe the houses of the Cistercian order were arranged the same way, in total contrast to the individual, not to say muddled, arrangements of the Irish tradition.

Grey Abbey   7 AUGUST 1815

Grey Abbey a Ruin near Mount Stewart   7 NOVEMBER 1809   Grey Abbey near Mt Stewart Co Down

Greyabbey seems to have been laid out on an ambitious scale which was later curtailed, leaving the nave aisleless and the cloister rectangular rather than square. The principal remains visible now and in the early nineteenth century are of the church with its array of pointed windows in the east wall and elaborate early-thirteenth-century west door. Kerr indicates that in his day the nave was still partially roofed, and in one instance turns the west gable towards the viewer to reveal the detail of its door, which he painstakingly records. The abbey belongs to the earliest phase of Gothic building style in Ireland. The pointed heads of the windows were visual effects to make the eye follow the lines of the building upwards rather than along its length. Mark Kerr has injected a whimsical note into his depiction of the west door by fashioning grass out of the name 'Grey Abbey'.

PORTAVO

Mark Kerr's drawing shows Portavo House from the sea, probably accomplished whilst aboard a craft kept in the boathouse beside the shore. It bears no date, but was perhaps done in 1815, during one of his visits to Mount Stewart. In early 1814, David Ker, the owner of Portavo, had married Selina Stewart, one of the daughters of Robert Stewart, Earl and subsequently 1st Marquess of Londonderry; as a result the lives of the two families became closely intermingled. In 1814, David and Selina joined Selina's half-brother, Lord Castlereagh, in London, and participated in the magnificent celebrations held to mark the defeat of Napoleon. Their young family spent much time at Mount Stewart, where they were doted upon by their elderly grandparents.

It would have been quite natural for Mark Kerr to visit the recently married couple, and inspect the progress of their new home, a substantial three-storey Palladian house over a raised, vaulted basement, the latter necessitated by the fact that it lay on a foundation of solid rock. The family's previous home formed an annexe to the new house. As Kerr's sketch shows, a three-bay pedimented projection on the entrance front gave the house an imposing air when viewed from the sea.

Selina's brother Charles, the future 3rd Marquess of Londonderry – a man not known for tact and moderation, nonetheless had a softer side where his family was concerned. On a visit to Portavo House in 1817, he found the building work far from complete. After wading through stones, bricks, heaps of compost and piles of lime mortar, he reached the hall, which, he thought, more than anything resembled an auction room, with pictures, statues, books and furniture piled on top of each other. Despite the chaotic conditions, his sister and her young family seemed happy, and he thought it better 'for others not to interfere when they can do no good'.

By 1819, the new house, known as 'the Castle', was finished. It was sumptuously furnished and hung with beautiful works of art. This house caught fire in 1844, and was subsequently replaced by another on a slightly different site. The remains of its raised basement still exists as a warren of stone tunnels and arches, with a number of stairways and entrances – the most enchanting place imaginable for hide-and-seek.

*King of Pugs: property of
Rt Honble Lady L Conolly*

CASTLETOWN HOUSE, COUNTY KILDARE

In the year of their marriage the newly-wedded Mark and Charlotte Kerr made their first visit to Ireland. A family celebration had been arranged in the splendid surroundings of Castletown House, County Kildare, the home of Thomas and Lady Louisa Connolly, to whom Mark Kerr was connected by marriage. This first journey to Ireland was negotiated via the Holyhead to Dunleary packet boat. Mark Kerr and the captain of this boat, MacGregor Skinner, became instant friends. The captain's brother, Cortland Skinner, was agent to Charlotte's half-brother. Years later, the Kerrs' eldest daughter, Letitia Louisa, having been the companion of firstly, Mark Kerr, and then Edmund McDonnell, following the death of their wives, would, aged over seventy, settle in the Isle of Wight to a life of married bliss with Cortland George MacGregor Skinner, Cortland Skinner's son.

The Castletown houseparty included Mark Kerr's eldest brother, Lord Ancram, his wife, Henrietta, and Lord Castlereagh and his wife, Emily, a Connolly relation and Lady Ancram's half-sister. Charlotte was by this time pregnant, and in Mark Kerr's drawings of Lady Louisa's pug dog, Bully, warming himself before the fire, one senses a longing for the comfortable domesticity that would shortly be theirs.

Castletown Bully Louisa Connolly   1799

99

Bully at Castletown   1799

The lovely Bully as A Fifer!

Their personal happiness must have been tempered to match the prevailing mood of the household, for the celebrations were taking place in the aftermath of the 1798 rebellion, which had had a profound effect on the Connolly family and Lady Louisa's sister's family, the Fitzgeralds, on the neighbouring estate at Carton. Louisa's nephew, Lord Edward Fitzgerald, one of the leaders of the insurrection, died in agony of septicaemia in June 1798, as a result of a wound inflicted during his arrest; and Louisa herself had been devastated by the disloyalty she had discovered amongst a household and tenantry on whom she had lavished forty years paternal concern and care. Her guests also had much to occupy their thoughts. Lord Ancram's regiment, the Midlothian Fencibles, was one of those sent to Ireland to quash the rebellion, and had taken part in the defeat of the French-led uprising in County Mayo; whilst Lord Castlereagh must have welcomed some respite from his long, difficult and still incomplete struggle to steer the Act of Union through the Irish Parliament. Even without his presence, the future course of Irish politics and Catholic emancipation would surely have been major topics of conversation.

Maynooth   28 SEPTEMBER 1811

MAYNOOTH CASTLE

Mark Kerr probably made this sketch whilst staying again at Castletown in 1811. Or perhaps it might have been done during an excursion to visit Lady Louisa Connolly's relations at nearby Carton. Part of the landscaping work carried out in conjunction with the rebuilding of Carton in 1739 was the construction of a broad straight street leading from the entrance gates towards the ruins of Maynooth Castle, thus linking a symbol of the Fitzgerald family's military past with one displaying its current affluent position in society.

In 1176 the manor of Maynooth was granted to Maurice Fitzgerald. He subsequently built the castle, which was to become the stronghold of the Norman Fitzgerald family for centuries and one of the principal fortresses of the Pale, the area around Dublin occupied by the Anglo-Irish By the late fourteenth century the Fitzgeralds were the most powerful family in the land.

In the centre of his drawing, Mark Kerr depicts the east (or south-east) tower, flanked by the gate tower and great tower. The south-east tower is just barely sketched in, and Kerr's depiction of its features, and indeed those of the other buildings, differs substantially from the existing masonry remains. Such inaccuracies may indicate that once again the drawing was worked up from a vague sketch made at the time. For instance, he shows the east and north walls of the great tower rising from a low point at the north-east angle, where the door is. At present this is the highest, not the lowest, point on the tower.

Cromlech Ireland

SELECT BIBLIOGRAPHY

Bell, Janet L., and T.E. McNeill, 'Bonamargy Friary, County Antrim', *Ulster Journal of Archaeology*, 61 (2002), 98–116

Bisset, William, 'Journal of a short tour in August 1799', ed. by the Very Rev. Dr Godfrey Brown, *The Glynns*, 33 (2005), 85–112

Boyd, Hugh A., 'Notes on Ballycastle in the Olden Days', *The Glynns*, 5 (1997), 5–10

Brett, C.E.B., *Buildings of County Antrim* (Belfast: Ulster Architectural Heritage Society and Ulster Historical Foundation, 1996)

Brett, C.E.B., *Buildings of North County Down* (Belfast: Ulster Architectural Heritage Society, 2002)

Brett, C.E.B., *Five Big Houses of Cushendun and Some Literary Associations* (Belfast: Lagan Press, 1997)

Brett, C.E.B., *Historic Buildings, Groups of Buildings, Areas of Architectural Importance in the Glens of Antrim* (Belfast: Ulster Architectural Heritage Society, 1970–71)

Brett, C.E.B., *Historic Buildings, Groups of Buildings, Areas of Architectural Importance in the Island of Rathlin* (Belfast: Ulster Architectural Heritage Society, 1974)

Carr, Peter, *Portavo: An Irish Townland and its Peoples*, 2 vols (Belfast: White Row Press, 2003 and 2005)

Casement, Anne, 'The Irish world of Lord Mark Kerr: consort of a countess, and admiral artist', *Irish Architectural and Decorative Studies*, 9 (2006), 40–85

Dallat, Cahal, *Antrim Coast & Glens A Personal View* (Belfast: HMSO, 1990)

Dallat, Cahal, 'Ballycastle's 18th Century Industries', *The Glynns,* 3 (1975), 7–13

Day, Angélique and Patrick McWilliams, eds, *Ordnance Survey Memoirs of Ireland Vol. 7, Parishes of County Down II 1832–4, 1837* (Belfast: Institute of Irish Studies, 1991) North Down & the Ards

Day, Angélique and Patrick McWilliams, eds, *Ordnance Survey Memoirs of Ireland Vol. 12, Parishes of County Down III 1833–8* (Belfast: Institute of Irish Studies, 1992) Mid-Down

Day, Angélique and Patrick McWilliams, eds, *Ordnance Survey Memoirs of Ireland Vol. 13, Parishes of County Antrim IV 1830–8* (Belfast: Institute of Irish Studies, 1992) Glens of Antrim

Day, Angélique and Patrick McWilliams, eds, *Ordnance Survey Memoirs of Ireland Vol. 16, Parishes of County Antrim V 1830–5, 1837–8* (Belfast: Institute of Irish Studies, 1992) Giant's Causeway and Ballymoney

Day, Angélique and Patrick McWilliams, eds, *Ordnance Survey Memoirs of Ireland Vol. 19, Parishes of County Antrim VI 1830, 1833, 1835–8* (Belfast: Institute of Irish Studies, 1993) South-West Antrim

Day, Angélique and Patrick McWilliams, eds, *Ordnance Survey Memoirs of Ireland Vol. 21, Parishes of County Antrim VII 1832–8* (Belfast: Institute of Irish Studies, 1993) South Antrim

Day, Angélique, Patrick McWilliams and Nóirín Dobson, eds, *Ordnance Survey Memoirs of Ireland Vol. 24, Parishes of County Antrim IX 1830-2, 1835, 1838–9* (Belfast: Institute of Irish Studies, 1994) North Antrim Coast and Rathlin

Day, Angélique, Patrick McWilliams and Nóirín Dobson, eds, *Ordnance Survey Memoirs of Ireland Vol. 26, Parishes of County Antrim X 1830–1, 1833–5, 1839–40* (Belfast: Institute of Irish Studies, 1994) East Antrim, Glynn, Inver, Kilroot and Templecorran

Day, Angélique and Patrick McWilliams, eds, *Ordnance Survey Memoirs of Ireland Vol. 29, Parishes of County Antrim XI 1832–3, 1835–9* (Belfast: Institute of Irish Studies, 1995) Antrim Town and Ballyclare

Day, Angélique, Patrick McWilliams, eds, *Ordnance Survey Memoirs of Ireland Vol. 32, Parishes of County Antrim XII 1832–3, 1835–40* (Belfast: Institute of Irish Studies, 1995) Ballynure and District

Day, Angélique, Patrick McWilliams and Lisa English, eds, *Ordnance Survey Memoirs of Ireland Vol. 33, Parishes of County Londonderry XII 1829–30, 1832, 1834–6* (Belfast: Institute of Irish Studies, 1995) Coleraine and Mouth of the Bann

Dobbs, Rev. Richard Stewart, 'Statistical Account of Ardclinis and Laid', in William Shaw Mason, *A Statistical Account or Parochial Survey of Ireland,* 3 vols (Dublin: Graisberry and Campbell and other presses, 1814–19) III (1819), 8–43

Dubourdieu, Rev. John, *Statistical Survey of the County of Antrim,* […], 2 vols (Dublin: Graisberry and Campbell, 1812)

Girvan, W.D., *Historic Buildings, Groups of Buildings, Areas of Architectural Importance in North Antrim including the Towns of Portrush, Ballymoney and Bushmills* (Belfast: Ulster Architectural Heritage Society, 1971–72)

Hamond, Fred, *Antrim Coast & Glens Industrial Heritage* (Belfast: HMSO, 1991)

Henry, Dean William, 'Topographical Description of the Coast of County Antrim and N. Down c.1740', annotated by Hugh Alexander Boyd, *The Glynns*, 2 (1974), 7–14

Hill, Rev. George, *An historical account of The MacDonnells of Antrim* […] (Belfast: Archer and Sons, 1873)

Irvine, Jimmy, 'The Old Coast Road from Larne to Ballycastle', *The Glynns*, 1 (1973), 16–20

Jope, E.M., ed., *An Archaeological Survey of County Down* (Belfast: HMSO, 1966)

McDonnell, Hector, *A History of Dunluce* (Belfast: Environment and Heritage Service, 2004)

McDonnell, Hector, *Irish Round Towers* (Glastonbury: Wooden Books, 2005)

McGill, Daniel J., *Col. Hugh Boyd's Ballycastle*, ed. by Gemma Reid (Coleraine: Causeway Museum Service, 2007)

McKillop, Felix, *Glenarm: A Local History* (Belfast: Ulster Journals, 1987)

McNeill, T.E., *Carrickfergus Castle, County Antrim* (Belfast: HMSO, 1981)

McNeill, T.E., *Castles in Ireland, feudal power in a Gaelic World* (London: Routledge, 2000)

McNeill, T.E., 'Excavations at Dunineny Castle, Co. Antrim', *Medieval Archaeology*, 48 (2004), 167–200.

McNeill, T.E., 'The Stone Castles of Northern County Antrim', *Ulster Journal of Archaeology*, 46 (1983), 101–28

McSparran, Malachy, 'The Mills of the Middle Glens', *The Glynns,* 4 (1976), 17–24

Magill, Paul, *Garron Tower, County Antrim* (Belfast: Paul Magill, 1990)

Mallory, J.P., and T.E. McNeill, *The Archaeology of Ulster from Colonization to Plantation* (Belfast: Institute of Irish Studies, 1991)

Montgomery, Ian, 'Drawing Blood from the Stones: the Giant's Causeway Case of 1897', *Familia*, 17 (2001), 65–86

Nicholl, Andrew, *Paintings of the Antrim Coast in 1828 with an introduction by Martyn Anglesea and historical and topographical notes by members of the Glens of Antrim Historical Society* (Belfast: Glens of Antrim Historical Society, 1982)

O'Laverty, Rev. James, *An Historical Account of the Diocese of Down and Connor, Ancient and Modern*, 5 vols (Dublin: James Duffy or M.H. Gill, 1878–1895)

Reeves-Smyth, Terence, 'Jewel of the Glen', *Irish Arts Review*, 23, no. 23 (Winter 2006), 126–31

Rhodes, P.S., *The Antrim Coast Road* (Belfast: Northern Ireland Tourist Board, n.d.)

Simon, Ben, ed., *A Treasured Landscape: the Heritage of Belvoir Park* (Belfast: The Forest of Belfast, 2005).

Smyth, Alastair, *The Story of Antrim* (Antrim: Antrim Borough Council, 1984)

Thackeray, William Makepeace, *The Irish Sketchbook and Critical Reviews* (London: John Murray, 1911)

Watson, Philip S., *A Companion To The Causeway Coast Way: A comprehensive guide to the walk from Portstewart to Ballycastle* (Belfast: Blackstaff Press, 2004)

Larne

Mt. Stewart. Greyabbey											25 OCTOBER

INDEX

Antrim Castle   72, 73
Antrim Coast Road 4–5
Antrim Motte   71
Antrim Round Tower   74–75
Ballycastle 28, 29, 30, 31, 37, 38, 39, 40
Ballymagarry 63
Ballymoney 64–65
Beardiville House 66
Belvoir Park, Newtownbreda 82–85
Birch Hill, Antrim 76
Bonamargy Friary 32–36
Broughanlea Cross, Ballycastle 44
Byfield Cottage, Antrim 77
Carrick-A-Rede 50–51
Carickfergus Castle 80–81
Castle Carra 24–25

Castletown House, County Kildare 99–100
Causeway Coast 57–59
Clare Park, Ballycastle 27
Clogh Castle 70
Culfeightrin Church, Glenshesk 42–43
Cushendall 23
Cushendun 26
Donaghadee 3
Dunluce Castle 60–62
Dunseverick Castle 52–53
Fair Head 41
Garron Point 18
Giant's Causeway 54–56
Glenarm Castle and Demesne 7–16
Glenariff 19
Greyabbey, County Down 96–97

Hillsborough 86
Kinbane Castle 47–49
Maynooth Castle 101
Maidens Lighthouses 6
Mount Stewart House and Demesne, County Down 87–92, 94–95
Nappan 17
Newtownards 93
Olderfleet Castle 79
Portavo 98
Portrush 67–69
Ram's Island, Lough Neagh 78
Rathlin Island 46
Red Bay 20, 21
Red Bay Castle 22
St Thomas's Church, Rathlin Island 45

The following images are reproduced courtesy of the Public Record Office of Northern Ireland

Page 4 Garron Point, Turnly's Pass
Page 6 The Maidens from the Shore Road
Page 9 Entrance to Glenarm Castle
Page 10 The Barbican at Glenarm
Page 12 Offices at Glenarm Castle; Corner of the Offices, Glenarm Castle
Page 13 Cottage in Glenarm Park October 1828
Page 14 Letitia, Marchioness of Antrim's Cottage
Page 15 In Glenarm River

Page 16 Fall in Glenarm Park; Fall in the River at Glenarm
Page 18 Pass cut through the Chalk Cliff Garron Point
Page 19 Glenariffe
Page 20 Pass Red Bay Castle
Page 22 Remains of Red Bay Castle
Page 23 Cushendall
Page 26 Cushendun Rocks; Cushendun – near the caves